HELMING
TO
WIN

I would like to say a huge thanks to Tim 'Garvinho' Garvin, my long suffering former crew, Keith Bedborough, and my even longer suffering wife, Emma, for their excellent input into drafts of this book. And a special thanks to Emma for allowing me the time to write this.

HELMING
TO
WIN

Nick Craig

FERNHURST
BOOKS

62 Brandon Parade, Holly Walk, Leamington Spa, Warwickshire, CV32 4JE, UK
Tel: +44 (0) 1926 337488 | www.fernhurstbooks.com

A catalogue record for this book is available from the British Library
ISBN 978-1-909911-22-2

Front cover image: *Nick Craig leading the 2014 RS400 Nationals at Mount's Bay* © Tom Gruitt
Back cover image: *Nick Craig winning the 2013 Endeavour Trophy at Burnham-on-Crouch* © Sue Pelling
All photographs © LPB Aerial Imagery, except:
p16, 23, 49, 50, 53, 56 © Jeremy Atkins; p45, 47 © Rachel Atkins; p13, 32, 36, 37, 39 © Tom Gruitt; p11, 13, 24, 30, 42, 50, 54, 55 © Alistair Mackay; p38, 61 © Tim Olin; p15 (Enterprise) by Peter Newton; p15 (Finn) by Steve Gregory; p15 (D-One) by Paul Williamson; p42 (OK) by Mary Reddyhoft

Fernhurst Books and Nick Craig would like to thank those who crewed on the photoshoots – Richard Lilley at Lymington Town Sailing Club and Toby Lewis at Draycote Water Sailing Club.

Designed and illustrated by Rachel Atkins
Printed in China through World Print

NICK CRAIG

CHAMPION OF CHAMPIONS

Nick Craig has won championships again and again in a variety of classes. So far he has achieved:

Single-hander (no spinnaker)
OK (4 x World Champion, European Champion, 8 x National Champion)
Finn (National Champion)
Phantom (National Champion)

Single-hander (asymmetric)
D-One (2 x World Champion, 2 x European Champion, 2 x National Champion)

Double-hander (no spinnaker)
Enterprise (3 x World Champion, 6 x National Champion)

Double-hander (symmetric spinnaker)
Merlin Rocket (National Champion)

Double-hander (asymmetric)
RS400 (8 x National Champion)
B14 (National Champion)

Team Racing
BUSA Championship (2 x Champion)

In total that is a remarkable 28 National championships, 8 European championships and 9 World championships... and counting! Few people can claim that number of championship wins and even fewer, if anyone, in so many different classes and types of boat. And to top this, Nick has won the UK's 'Champion of Champions' event (The Endeavour Trophy) 6 times – more than any other sailor. And this has all been done while holding down a full-time job!

It is no wonder that Nick was awarded the YJA *Yachtsman of the Year* in 2011 and the Yachts & Yachting *Amateur Sailor of the Year* in 2013.

Helming to Win is, in many ways, Nick's personal journey from club racer to championship winner. With this book, and enough dedication, you too can become a champion!

CONTENTS

FOREWORD

Nick Craig is the outstanding amateur sailor of his generation. To achieve what he has done in such a variety of classes, while holding down a full-time job, is remarkable.

Having raced against Nick a number of times, I can say that he is one of the best. He has been so successful by really understanding what makes a boat sail fast and applying this on the race course. This book allows anyone to gain from his experiences.

In my own journey from club racing my Optimist to winning major championships I have deployed a lot of the techniques that Nick describes. Anyone reading this book will greatly accelerate their learning curve and be taking an important step to achieving their own championship objectives.

Sir Ben Ainslie
4 x Olympic gold medallist, 1 x America's Cup winner

LEARNING TO WIN

Ingredients for Winning

Sailing is arguably the world's greatest sport because its complexity and variety mean that it can be pursued for life without boredom or repetitiveness. However, while sailing is complex, it can be broken down into a series of processes that can be perfected with focused training. With the right amount of time, commitment and mindset, everyone can take their sailing up a few gears.

There are eight key skill areas that need to be strong to win sailing championships:

This book will focus on the first three of these, while other books in the *Sail to Win* series provide more detailed thinking on the remaining skill areas.

But firstly some brief pointers on the 5 skill areas that aren't covered in depth in this book:

Strategy

Picking the right strategy (i.e. the paying way up a beat or downwind) is all about information gathering. No one knows which side will pay on a leg but a tactician's objective is to get this decision right as often as possible by gathering every bit of information to make a well-informed choice. No one gets this right all of the time so it is vital to analyse and learn from your mistakes. Bias of the first beat to one tack or another, the windshift pattern, wind bends, potential sea breeze influence, wave pattern, tide and history should all play a role in the judgement you make on which side of the beat may pay.

How far you head to one side of the course depends on how strongly your analysis points to that side of the course and your attitude to risk for that race. Early in a series, a low risk strategy generally makes sense as you look for some early counters in your scoreline. Later in the series your attitude to risk will depend on how you are doing versus your objectives. If you are ahead of your personal objectives, then a low risk strategy should continue to make sense. If you are behind your objectives, it may be time to take more risk.

Boat-on-Boat Tactics

In order to hone your tactics, race in high quality fleets in tight situations, or try some match or team racing. Planning a move, or several moves, ahead is key for boat-on-boat tactics.

Getting on the right hand side of your opposition often works, giving you the favourable starboard tack when things are close.

Those on the right hand side have the favoured starboard tack

Downwind it often pays to work the side that will give you an inside overlap at the next mark.

3685 has gone left and got an inside overlap

Mental Strength

Mental strength is a very individual thing. Everyone has an unconscious mind which provides continuous chatter that is not always helpful. If you find yourself disagreeing that you have an unconscious mind, your unconscious mind is clearly talking to you! That 'chatter' is often the source of negative thoughts, e.g. "Don't capsize at this gybe mark, you're doing really well!" A key skill is replacing any negative thoughts as soon as they enter your head with positive ones.

Another approach is to distract that wandering mind. There is a lot going on in sailing, so focusing on the wind, waves and opposition is usually enough to distract even the most active wandering mind!

Rules Knowledge

Reading the Rule Book isn't a great way to learn the rules as they are dry, long and sometimes seemingly contradictory, and it is hard to interpret them without knowing which rules override others. Bryan Willis' *Rules in Practice* is excellent at making those interpretations while also providing the relevant rule for every situation. After an incident on the water, always refer to the Rule Book or *Rules In Practice* to ensure that you have fully understood the situation. You are much more likely to remember the relevant rule after a live incident.

The sailing rules aren't as fair as a court of law. There are situations where you are guilty until proven innocent: e.g. as windward boat, port tack boat, and when breaking or establishing an overlap when denying or claiming water at a mark. So, in these situations, you may need to exercise more caution depending on your attitude to risk at that point in the event.

In general, it pays to steer clear of trouble. There are few protests between leading sailors and a healthy give and take attitude – top sailors will tend to let a misjudgement on a close situation go – in the knowledge that at some point it will payback.

> *At the 2003 Enterprise Worlds we were stuck behind a slower boat on a reach. We went high to overtake and were about to break clear after around 45 seconds (a quick overtake in an Enterprise!) when the leeward boat luffed as hard as they could and made a dent in the gunwale of my lovely wooden boat. I shouted protest and had two witnesses supporting my claim that the leeward boat hadn't given us time and opportunity to avoid a collision. We lost the protest. The key learning from this is that as windward boat (and in several other scenarios), you are guilty until proven innocent. The protest committee noted that we had been overlapped for 45 seconds, so, in their view, had ample time and opportunity to avoid a collision.*

Physical Fitness

Fitness is really important if you have perfected the other seven skill areas. Being super-fit but a weak starter, or not knowing how to make a boat go fast, won't help that much. But once you have mastered all of these other areas, fitness plays a key part in gaining an edge versus other strong all-round sailors. Variety, and making fitness part of your daily routine, can ensure fitness becomes your friend for life. Provided the exercise is intense, 30 minutes a day is sufficient to get pretty fit, though more is good to build stamina and strength. The best fitness for sailing is windy weather sailing, but often that is a rare treat. Good substitutes are cycling, rowing machine, circuits and swimming, probably in that order, though that varies by boat and what your job is in the boat.

And not forgetting... The Crew

Looking beyond the eight key skill areas, your crew is your most important winning ingredient (unless you sail a single-hander!). You should ideally sail with the best crew possible who is a match with your expectations, time requirements and competitiveness. If you are highly competitive, it is important to have a crew with a similar mindset. If you are very relaxed about your results, you should sail with someone who is equally chilled out.

Accelerating your Learning
Curve

Sailing success is probably 5% talent and 95% hard work. 'Hard work' = lots of hours on the water, but, more importantly, making the most of that time. This section provides some pointers on how to ensure your time on the water is quality time.

There are 5 key approaches that will help make the most of your time on the water:

1 Sail Against 'The Best'

2 Variety of Classes

3 'Training' v. 'Win' Events

4 Learning Objectives

5 Consolidate Learning

1. Sail Against 'The Best'

Always aim to sail against the best sailors, ideally in fleets where the standard is high and above your own. Sailing against better sailors than yourself will sharpen you up as you will need to nail the start and hold difficult lanes effectively (more on that later) to avoid being swallowed up by the pack in the first few hundred metres of the race. But more importantly, observing and talking to top sailors is a great way to learn – and it is fun!

2. Variety of Classes

Sailing against different people at different venues is a great way to learn. Techniques from different classes can be re-applied across classes, meaning that you come back to your original class a better sailor. It is easy to get stale sailing one boat so, where possible, gaining a variety of experiences is hugely valuable. If possible that experience should

The lessons you will learn through sailing a variety of classes can be re-applied to your original class

include dinghies, cats and yachts, plus fleet, match and team racing, as each require different skills and provide new insights into the sport.

In the short term, sailing a variety of classes can be frustrating as you will be slower than you are used to in your new class. Mixing your boats will also initially slow you down in your main class as you lose some feel for it. But, in the long term, you will become a much better sailor, and can always re-gain the feel for your main class by putting the hours back into your chosen class again.

3. 'Training' v. 'Win' Events

'Training' events are those where your aim is to learn as much as possible, rather than to win or necessarily do well. The more training events you build into your season, the faster you will learn. You should still be giving it your all at training events, even though you don't have an outcome goal.

Training events can be quite tough as you need to swallow your ego and accept that you may not do well if some of the things you are trying don't work. But, in the long term, you will learn more and become a better sailor. You can generally still do pretty well, or even better than usual, at training events with this approach, as some of your experiments *will* work.

Another benefit of incorporating training events into your season is that they make the 'win' events, where you stop experimenting, in many ways easier than the training events. You drop the distraction of trying new things so you have less to think about and can keep things simple. This can also give the impression that you sail better under pressure as your performance moves up a gear at the main events, giving you an important psychological edge.

To accelerate your learning curve even further, be prepared to turn a win event into a training event if results aren't going to plan. A few beers always help with this transition!

This is a key approach to developing your sailing. Countless sailors race week-in week-out but never improve because they hit a plateau and routine which they don't seek to break or improve upon. They are putting the hours in, but they aren't quality hours.

4. Learning Objectives

Set 3-5 learning objectives at training events. For example:
1. Boatspeed (adjusting one variable at a time).
2. Starts (get out your comfort zone – aim to start at the part of the line where you are least comfortable and generally find yourself having most issues).
3. Process (e.g. head out of the boat, i.e. looking around, rather than at your feet or telltales).
4. Boat handling (e.g. pressure test your boat handling by gybing on every gust when it's windy).

Learning Objective 2: Push yourself in training events, e.g. attempt a dramatically different start

Learning Objective 4: Improve your boat handling skills, e.g. by gybing on every gust when it is windy

5. Consolidate Learning

Replay the tape & take notes. After a race, replay as much of the race as you can in your head, focusing on any situation where you lost distance. Also focus on when you were fast and remember how it feels so that you know what you are searching for in future. Make notes for future reference and review those notes before your next sail to help create your next set of learning objectives. This is a great constructive discussion to have with your crew.

> **TOP TIP**
>
> Some of these approaches take time and money, so you should devise a season plan within the time and financial constraints you have. Focus on racing that offers the best competition, pick your training events (as many as possible) and build in a variety of classes if possible. To peak in a single boat you need to focus on that class, but in the long term variety is good.

This sounds like a regimented approach but a lot of fun and satisfaction can be had out of this continuous learning evolution, as well as the joy of sailboat racing! You should understand your own strengths and weaknesses and which types of sailing better address those areas. Sailing at events will help your tactics and starts. But you also need some time two-boat tuning and should be willing to miss events to do that to improve your boatspeed. And you also need time on your own to perfect your boat handling and starts via slow speed boat handling practice.

66 *If you are limited for time, you need to focus your training more. For the last few RS400 Nationals we have had minimal time to prepare as I'm doing less sailing with family commitments, and I've been campaigning in other boats. We are confident in our speed from many years of RS400 sailing and a season of intense two-boat tuning. So we spend the limited time we have on sharpening up our boat handling by sailing alone in the evening at Lee on the Solent. The Solent is great for this as the choppy waves make boat handling tricky. And we squeeze in some racing practice if possible.* 99

Practising in the Solent chop is a great way of sharpening boat handling skills

Where to Look when Racing

When you first start sailing, or are new to a boat, you tend to look at your feet to ensure that you aren't tripping up. The key to progressing is looking further and further up and knowing when to switch between the modes.

Broadly, there are 5 modes (places to look):

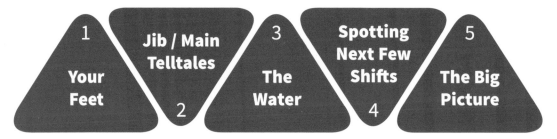

1 Your Feet

Jib / Main Telltales 2

3 The Water

Spotting Next Few Shifts 4

5 The Big Picture

Mode 1: Your Feet

This is inevitable when you are new to the sport or a boat. It is an appropriate place to look when your boat handling is being pushed to its limit. Your boat handling limit will, of course, vary depending on how experienced you are in your chosen boat. However, you will miss a lot of windshifts and gusts if you look down too much.

You should move away from this mode as soon as possible, partly through being aware of where you are looking and by forcing yourself to look up. That can be hard as it may be outside your comfort zone and may mean that you fall over, or even out of the boat, occasionally, but it is a good thing to do at those training events.

Mode 2: Jib / Main Telltales

100% concentration on your telltales ensures that you are dead on the wind all of the time upwind and that your sails are always set optimally downwind. This is a good mode when boatspeed is critical, e.g. in a tight spot out of a start. However, you should eventually be able to keep your boat dead on the wind (or keep the sails optimally set) without spending much time staring at the telltales. Again, practice is key for this, forcing yourself to look at the water and not the jib is a good discipline.

> **TOP TIP**
>
> Sailing with your eyes shut works well in a two-man boat where the crew can guide the helm. This is a useful exercise for making sailing optimally instinctive.

Mode 3: The Water

This is the most important step to move you from reactive to proactive sailing. By looking at the water you can spot gusts and the angle that they are moving towards you (by looking at the angle of the ripples on the water and the direction of travel of the gust).

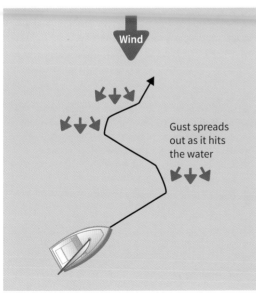

Gust spreading out

As gusts hit the water they fan out, just as an egg dropped on the ground does. So looking upwind on starboard tack, there is a lift on starboard to the left of the gust and a header on starboard to the right. This is especially pronounced where there are obstacles around your sailing water so the wind is bouncing down from height, e.g. at Frensham Pond, where I grew up and learnt to wind spot.

The diagram may suggest that this is predictable... but gust spotting is a black art because every gust / lull is different and changing (but this makes sailing hard and interesting!).

The more time you spend gust spotting, the better you get at it. By knowing how strong and at what angle the next gust will hit, you can set your boat up and steer just before it hits to make the most of the gust so that it accelerates you rather than causes you to heel. Doing this, and consequently sailing consistently flat, is the biggest jump in speed most sailors can make. And it is free! With practice this will become reasonably automatic so that you can look further up to the next few shifts...

Mode 4: Spotting Next Few Shifts

This is a key step to being able to consistently pick shifts well. By looking further up the course and looking at the direction that the next few shifts are coming down the course, you can map your next few tacks / gybes / downwind steering. By doing this you are making a proactive plan, rather than reacting to the shifts as they come in.

Mode 5: The Big Picture

With enough practice, modes 1-4 become more instinctive and you can focus on the big picture; looking at where you are relative to the fleet, what the clouds are doing and which side of the course the gaining boats have come from.

There is an enormous amount to look for when sailing. Making as much of this as instinctive as possible is the key to success and the reason why no

You can focus on the bigger picture when modes 1-4 become instinctive

one reaches the top level in sailing without many years of quality time on the water.

The ideal approach is to be able to sail in modes 4 and 5 most of the time, with modes 1, 2 and 3 coming instinctively through many hours of quality practice. With practice, your boat handling will be slick without looking at your feet, you can sail your boat fast without looking at the telltales, and a fleeting glance will give you enough perspective to know what the near term gusts, lulls and shifts are doing.

Top sailors are better at spotting shifts because they have the time to look for them since so much of their game has become instinctive. By spending more time looking for them, they also get better at spotting the subtle patterns in the water which indicate a gust / lull or header / lift, and so have better gust response and route planning.

Knowing when to switch between the modes is a powerful tool:
- If you get a great start, move quickly to **mode 5** to assess how to consolidate that lead.
- If you are struggling to find a lane out of a mediocre start, move to **mode 2**.
- If you are sailing on a gusty lake and approaching the windward mark on a layline, modes 4 and 5 are largely irrelevant, so switch to **mode 3**.
- If you feel you've lost the rhythm of the windshifts, shift to **mode 4**.

An aware crew plays a key role in this. By knowing or communicating with the helm to understand which mode they are in, the crew can focus on other areas. For example, if the helm is in mode 2 focusing on speed, the crew can be in mode 5.

This may sound like a very complex process. With enough quality racing, switching between these modes also becomes instinctive, just as watching a toddler learn to walk is pretty painful but they get there in the end!

> 66 *At the 2013 D-One Nationals I had been out of the boat for a while. I was complacent about that and spent my time trying to be in modes 4 and 5. I fell out of the boat during a tight tack into the windward mark! This cost me the two points which went on to lose me the Nationals. I should have recognised my lack of time in the boat and spent a little more time in mode 1!* 99

TOP TIP

The one place you shouldn't be looking is at your burgee. The burgee tells you what has just happened. You won't be able to sail proactively looking at wind history! Sailing without a burgee eliminates this distraction, takes away a key tool from your opposition for knowing where your dirty air range is and marginally reduces weight just where you don't want it, i.e. high up (which increases pitching).

SAILING FAST IN A STRAIGHT LINE

PART 2

How to Get Fast!

In most classes, boatspeed is down to 5% static settings, 20% dynamic settings and 75% technique. Yet the focus of 'dinghy park chat' is mainly about static settings!

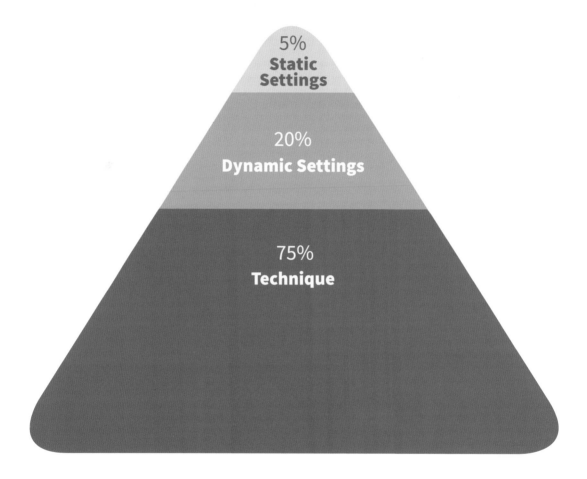

5%
Static Settings

20%
Dynamic Settings

75%
Technique

Static Settings

Static settings are those that you set up on shore, e.g. mast rake, spreaders, rig tension (in most boats), etc.

You will be very slow if your static settings are wrong. However, it is easy to have these in the right ballpark by copying the settings of the top sailors in your class. Generally, these are readily available online or from a friendly sailmaker. It takes a lot of experimentation and two-boat tuning to find numbers that work better than these. So, unless you've mastered everything else about your boat, the best bet is to copy the settings of the top boats and then forget about static settings and focus on the other 95% that contributes to boatspeed.

Dynamic Settings

Your dynamic settings are those that you adjust on the water. Knowing how to set these and, importantly, adjust these as conditions change ('changing gears') is very important.

The key dynamic levers in most boats are sheet tension, kicker, traveller, centreboard and cunningham, quite often in that order. However, the key dynamic levers, and their importance, vary by class. For example, in a Finn / D-One / OK the key levers are sheet tension and traveller; in the Merlin Rocket they are mast rake, centreboard and kicker; in an Enterprise or B14 they are sheet tension & kicker (but very different amounts).

Know how to adjust the key dynamic levers

You can work out which dynamic levers are key in your class, and how much to use them, by:
1. Talking to the top sailors in your class.
2. Observing the top sailors in your class sailing and then asking them questions.

3. Outside of racing, go too heavy or light on each dynamic setting in turn to develop a feel for what that does to weather helm and power.
4. When racing, do the same but within a narrower range to see what works and what does not.
5. Two-boat tuning.

All of this takes a lot of time. Every sailing day is a little different in wind strength, gustiness and wave pattern. With that, the optimal dynamic settings will vary somewhat. Plus there are multiple combinations of settings so the possible combinations are large (but finite). However, this is time well invested. Once you work out what makes your boat tick, it will give you a permanent jump in speed that you can always rely on and is very hard for others to replicate. While static settings are easy to copy, copying dynamic settings is much harder. Note taking should be a key part of this learning process. With time in your boat, knowing the right dynamic settings will become second nature rather than being a note taking exercise. However, that will only happen if you do experiment and do not sail with the same set up every week.

Working these settings effectively and changing gears through conditions is a mixture of feel and numbers. While some sailors may have a more innate feel than others, a feel for the right settings can certainly be learnt through quality time in a boat.

This book doesn't aim to cover the theory behind different rig set ups and tuning. However, that is worth knowing as it will greatly accelerate your learning curve by giving you an idea of which settings, and combinations of those, might work.

Use this sequence to work out which dynamic levers are most important for your class

You should aim to develop a set of 'base' settings for each condition in your class of boat. At big events you can then quickly slot into these and focus on other things. At training events you should look to change one thing at a time from these base settings and, if the change proves fast, adjust your base settings. Through this iterative process you should always be moving your boatspeed forward.

Whilst this is largely personal preference and there are different approaches, I like having numbers to reference for static settings, whereas I don't mark ropes or seek to generate numbers for dynamic settings. For dynamic settings, it is important to develop an eye for your sails and a feel for your boat so that you can judge what works well. The wind and wave state is highly dynamic so I personally think that reference numbers for dynamic settings are of limited use.

Tuning Partners

Your ideal tuning partner is slightly faster than you so that you can raise your game. However, that is often hard to find and may not meet the objectives of your partner who will also be looking for someone faster! Finding someone with strengths in different conditions to yourself can be a good fit. Even if you can only find someone slower than you in all conditions to tune with, that can still be very powerful. By putting yourself in awkward starting positions in tuning runs, a slower tuning partner can still force you to sail faster and learn to hold lanes in difficult situations.

Experimenting

In the absence of a tuning partner, you can learn a lot about how the dynamic settings work for your boat by experimenting. You should initially start with a wide range, adjusting one control at a time to see its effect. You should try these changes across conditions, and for a reasonable amount of time, to see whether they work. Don't be afraid to do this while racing, and effectively use the boats you are racing against as tuning aids. As you get to know your boat better, you can narrow the range in which you are experimenting.

66 *My judgement is that it takes 30 days in the same conditions to learn to sail fast in a boat. Given that there are, say, 15 different wind / wave states, if you sail every other weekend, it will take 9 years to get fully up to speed in a boat.*

This was really brought home to me at the 2003 OK World Championships in India. I went there having done a lot of OK sailing and felt confident that this could be my year after several top three finishes but never a win. The international fleet were trounced by an Indian, Nitin Mongia, who finished in the 20s at the previous Worlds. He was quicker up and downwind and won nearly every race. How did he do it?

He had done around a month of training before the event. During the event the thermal conditions at the venue were virtually identical every day – and so the conditions that he had practised in for 30 days were the conditions that he went on to race in. Training in more varied conditions myself, it would have taken 9 years on my simple maths to get as quick as Nitin in those conditions. (That's what I like to tell myself anyway!) 99

Your ideal tuning partner is slightly faster than you, but so is theirs!

Upwind Speed

The key reason why some people seem to be able to sail fast in any boat is good technique. Good technique means being able to sail a boat consistently flat and balanced as the wind changes in strength and direction with minimal use of the rudder. Often this is described as being 'in the groove'. Upwind speed is achieved by setting your boat up correctly and sailing it flat.

Getting 'In The Groove'

Sailing 'in the groove' is a wonderful feeling – you feel your boat sailing higher and faster than those around you.

Your boat is 'in the groove' when:
1. It is dead flat in all sea states.
2. Your foils are providing lift, as shown by slight weather helm (i.e. the boat tries to point to windward a touch when sailed flat).
3. Your sails are optimally set for the wind and wave conditions (which is a book in itself!).

Sailing Flat

Your boat needs to be sailed dead flat to be 'in the groove'. This is an unnatural position unless you have trained yourself to sail like this, because a few degrees of heel is more comfortable. An inclinometer (showing your angle of heel) is a useful training aid, and it is also helpful to look behind at the ripples from the rudder to see that they are even. Sailing consistently flat is much harder than sailing flat momentarily. To do it consistently you need to be anticipating the heeling effect of gusts and lulls which can only be achieved by having your head out of the boat.

In training, and in training events, a good objective is to sail flat all of the time. This may slow you up at first because you may be focusing on this rather than your telltales, the next gust or the multitude of other things that sailors can be looking for. But be persistent and eventually sailing flat will become a habit which you don't need to concentrate on. It is then a lifetime skill which will give you a permanent edge over most sailors. Sailing consistently flat is the biggest jump in speed most sailors can make, and the cheapest way to increase boatspeed!

Sailing flat, not even slightly heeled, is the biggest jump in speed most sailors can make

Foils / Feel on The Tiller

The tiller is a vital feedback loop for the helm. So you must treat it nicely and hold it lightly so that the boat can 'talk' to you. On most boats you are aiming for a touch of weather helm, i.e. a little bit of pull to leeward on the tiller. It does vary by boat, for example a Merlin Rocket likes a very light tiller, an OK a heavier one. Spending time letting the boat talk to you with a light grip on the tiller extension will increase your feel for your boat.

Your foils should be just biting (shown by slight weather helm), thus generating lift. However, you don't want your foils to bite too hard or you will be having to pull your tiller towards you all the time to stop your boat luffing. This creates a lot of drag from your rudder.

> **TOP TIP**
>
> If you feel you have fallen out of the groove, it is natural to tense up which normally means gripping the tiller extension tighter. You then feel the boat less and can enter a vicious circle of slowness! If you feel you are out of the groove, put the tiller extension behind you (the 'frying pan' grip) and grip it lightly so that you regain feel of your boat.

Normal grip on tiller

'Frying pan' grip on tiller

Sails

Your sails should be optimally set with all telltales flowing or just breaking and your sails set to the optimal shape for the conditions.

The Dynamic Groove

Most boats have a 'high' and 'low' groove. The high groove is when the boat sails really fast being pinched a touch; the low groove is when it is sailed low, fast and free. Finding these two grooves for your boat is a really powerful tactical weapon.

Typically the high mode will mean tighter leeches and a flatter luff entry. So you should sail with a touch more mainsheet tension / kicker and a touch less outhaul and inhaul to move the draft aft and hook the lower leech. You should also sail with a touch more leeward heel and look for height via a touch of pinching in flat spots of water. All of these adjustments are subtle compared to the low mode.

The low groove typically means setting up with slightly more open leeches and a rounder luff entry. You should sail with a touch less mainsheet tension / kicker and a touch more inhaul to open up the luff entry so that your boat naturally points lower. You may use a little more outhaul to open up the lower leech. If it is windy, you will have to play the sails much more because you aren't using pinching to take the sting out of gusts. Again, all of these changes are subtle compared to high mode, except for the amount of mainsheet movement.

Keeping a boat consistently 'in the groove' as the wind and waves change is much harder than initially finding the groove. It is the key reason why some people can sail a range of boats consistently fast. The secrets are stability of heel, suitable tiller movement and the ability to change gears.

Stability of Heel

To be 'in the groove', your boat needs to be flat and, more importantly, consistently flat. Stability of heel is key. If your boat is wobbling from side to side you will upset the flow over the foils, which is critical to generating lift. Stability of heel will generate more lift and enable you to sail higher than the boats around you, with no loss of speed. It is the secret weapon for 'pointing high'.

Delivering stability of heel requires anticipation of gusts and lulls so that you can be proactive in adjusting your hiking and sail settings ahead of the change in the wind, thus keeping your boat flat. Sailing with your head out of the boat and an excellent crew are critical for this. All of that practice at sailing with your head out of the boat doesn't just make you better at spotting windshifts, it also enables you to sail your boat faster. So even a light wind day can be a workout if it is gusty!

Tiller Movement

Your tiller movement should match the pattern of the wind and waves for that day. So if the waves are short and choppy, and the wind is gusty, your tiller movement can be more dynamic. If the water is flat, and the wind steady, your tiller movements should be minimal.

Changing Gears

You need to transition between these states as often as the wind dictates. On a gusty day, you may need to change your rig set up often, and less so when the wind is more stable. You should aim to be able to change your rig set up and steering style quickly as the breeze changes whilst maintaining stability of heel.

> 66 *Staying in the 'dynamic groove' is really hard to do, especially in shifty, gusty conditions as that groove is on the move. Finn sailing on the Olympic circuit taught me just how good some sailors are at doing this. Racing a Finn at this level was like running up a fast moving escalator! In most amateur fleets, if you can slot your boat 'in the groove' you are moving forwards versus the fleet. In the Finn, if you weren't 'in the groove' you were going backwards, making it tough at times just to get away from the start line without being spat out the back. The top Finn sailors are 'in the groove' 90-100% of the time.* 99

Upwind in Flat Water

Rig Set Up for Height

With flat water sailing, there are no waves to slow you down if you try to sail high. The limit on height is stalling the foils and your sails not working efficiently (because you are sailing inside the narrowest angle to the wind that your rig set up allows).

This is a trade-off – it is worth losing a little speed for more height. This trade-off varies by class. Generally, faster boats with narrower foils don't like being pinched and vice versa. So an Enterprise with fat foils and a low speed loves being pinched. A Finn and Lark with thin foils struggle with pinching, and it rarely works in skiffs upwind.

You should be sailing your boat on a 'knife edge' of height in these conditions – your foils should be on the edge of stalling. You can always sail higher by pinching more but at some point (which varies by class) you will lose flow on your foils and so lose speed and lift. It takes practice at sailing too high to know where that stall point is in your boat across different conditions. With time, this can become an innate skill that you don't have to think about.

A key point is that you should set up your boat for height mainly through rig set up rather than steering. The boat should want to naturally sail high or you will be dragging your rudder round if you are consistently slightly luffing to point high.

Smooth Steering

With no waves to steer around, your steering should be smooth inland. You should maintain a light tiller extension grip and consider adopting the 'frying pan' steering style (tiller extension to the aft side of your body) in light winds to ensure really smooth steering. As much as possible you should be using body movement and sail trim to steer.

When to Take Height

Being high and fast is every sailor's upwind dream. The best time to take height is just before sharp gusts hit so that you take out the impact that would have heeled you and you don't go sideways. It is vital to look out of the boat to anticipate the gusts and time that pinch.

Dynamic Sail Trim & Sideways Body Movement

Your sail trim should match the intensity and frequency of the wind. So, if the wind is light and stable, your sail trim should be delicate and small. If the wind is strong and gusty, your sail trim should be heavy and aggressive. That can mean sailing in an ambidextrous mode! So, if it is flat water but very gusty, your tiller hand needs to be steering smoothly whilst your mainsheet hand needs to be aggressive. Taking a bit of time before the start of each day's racing to work out what the conditions are and what sailing style will suit that day is time well spent.

Upwind in Waves

Rig Set Up for Speed

In waves you need more drive and acceleration, rather than height. You should set your rig up so that the boat naturally wants to point lower and accelerate quickly after you hit waves. This generally means moving the fullness forward in your sails so that your boat naturally points a little lower. This can be helped by moving the mast step forward (if possible). You should also sail with slightly more open leeches to enable acceleration. This is typically achieved by a little more inhaul and a little less kicker and sheet tension, and by pulling on the cunningham a little earlier than on flat water. These changes should be small compared to your inland settings.

Steer to Match the Waves

Your steering should match the frequency and shape of the waves. So if the waves are long and smooth, your steering should be slow and smooth. If the waves are close together and choppy, your steering should be faster and more punchy. You should aim to adapt your steering to every upcoming wave pattern. At first this takes

a huge conscious effort but, with many hours on the water, this will become second nature and you can focus on other things. In general, most sailors new to waves over-steer with the rudder. As much of the steering as possible should be done with legitimate body movement and sail trim.

When to Take Height

While it generally pays to sail lower in waves than inland, it is still preferable to be faster and higher on the sea! The trick is taking height between the waves where there are flat spots. So you are effectively moving back into flat water mode when the opportunity arises. If your boat has a traveller, moving this up during flat spots can also be a useful trick for gaining height.

Sail Trim & Multi-Directional Body Movement

Body movement is the key to boatspeed in waves. As you luff up waves and bear off down them you should ideally do that steering via sail trim and body movement. Most of your upwind body movement is through moving your upper body forwards and backwards in time with the waves. For really big waves, you may also slide your backside forwards and backwards.

Your fore-aft body movement should match the size and frequency of the waves. So if the waves are long and smooth, your body movement should match that. If the waves are short and choppy, your body movement needs to be fast and punchy. In general, upper body movement is sufficient. For choppy, tricky waves, a little bit of leeward heel can help to increase the pressure on your foils to keep the flow attached.

Effective fore-aft body movement means that you have to steer less around waves resulting in more speed and height.

Your objective should be that the bow of your boat sticks smoothly to the waves irrespective of the sea state. This is potentially very hard work in chop and on windy days. The top Finn sailors do this over every wave, but they are full-time athletes! You should aim to be able to do this and use it at key times in the race, e.g. out of the start.

Body movement is key to boatspeed in waves

Upwind in Light Winds
(Sub-powered)

Heel

You should ideally still sail your boat flat in light winds or you are presenting a sub-optimal, skewed hull shape to the water. If you need some leeward heel to get lift off the foils, see if you can generate that lift though moving your rig aft and / or moving the centreboard forwards. Both of these help to move the centre of effort or push point (the central point of the force from your sails) aft of the centre of lateral resistance or pivot point (the point that your boat turns around).

It is easier to get the foils working with some leeward heel, but it is faster to have a flat boat and the foils working. However, some leeward heel can be beneficial when it is very challenging to get the boat 'in the groove', e.g. in light winds and chop.

In a drifter, quite a bit of leeward heel can pay because it reduces the wetted surface area of your hull and enables gravity to pull some shape into your sails. Alternatively, you can visit the bar!

Tightening up your toestraps in light winds enables you to get on your toestraps early – which gives you more feel for the boat, provides the boat with more inertia through the waves and tricks your opposition into thinking you are sailing in more wind than them! Adjustable toestraps are a must, provided they are class legal.

Trim

Simply put, the front half of most boats are designed to cut through water effectively, and the back half to surf. So in lighter winds you should be sitting further forward to cut through water more effectively and reduce the wetted surface area of your boat by slightly lifting the flat surfboard-shaped aft end of the boat out the water.

Rig Set Up

You are looking to set up your rig for maximum power. Generally this means upright mast rake, as deep sails as possible, without the air flow over them stalling, and the main and jib shape matching and so working together.

Sail Trim

You are seeking to avoid over-sheeting so that your leech has room to breathe. However, the first sailors to sheet in and take up the luff curve in their mainsail (the mainsheet tension induces mast bend and moves the draft aft) are typically quickest. You should be operating on a knife edge between stalling your leech and having too full a luff, especially on rigs with lots of luff curve.

Aim for pretty flat sails until the wind has sufficient energy to get over larger curves and produce more power from your rig. This typically only requires 5 knots or so of wind to move to fuller sails and the search for power (until you are overpowered).

Body Positioning

Ideally helm and crew weight should be close together to reduce windage. This isn't always possible in light winds. Spotting wind is crucial for both helm and crew in fickle breezes. So it generally pays to have at least the helm up on the windward sidedeck and the crew counterbalancing to allow the helm to be high up looking around for breeze. Your movements should be gentle and smooth in light airs; the wind has very little energy so is easily 'knocked off' the sails.

Sitting forward in a drifter

Upwind in Medium Winds
(Full Power)

Heel

In general, it pays to sail your boat dead flat. A little bit of leeward heel can pay in nasty chop but that heel needs to be stable to maintain flow over the foils.

Trim

You should sit further back (compared to light winds). As a rough guide your bow will just be cutting through the water.

Rig Set Up

You are looking for maximum power from your rig. This will generally mean upright mast rake and spreaders, and rig tension / lowers set up for maximum power. Numbers on this vary by class so it is best to refer to tuning guides and experiment from there.

Sail Trim

In medium airs, it generally pays to have fairly powerful, full sails and relatively tight leeches. It can be as hard work upwind as in windy weather because sailing in medium winds is probably when you will use most mainsheet load.

Body Positioning

The crew should be more outboard than the helm so that the helm has a clear view of the jib and the water. The helm should move all the way inboard so that they are nearly falling off the inner edge of side deck to keep the crew outboard. When the helm can no longer just perch on the sidedeck without inducing windward heel, the helm and crew should swap with the helm moving outboard into a more normal position. With the helm moving outboard significantly, the crew has to move in more to ensure that the helm's view is not obstructed. That swap is a significant and distracting movement so keep it to a minimum. You can minimise these swaps by increasing the helm's range of movement from perched on the inner edge of the sidedeck to fully hiked. With the

helm perched on the inner edge of the sidedeck, you can be the first to have your crew hiking, so it looks like you are sailing in more wind or have a better rig set up than your opposition!

When you are just on the edge of being overpowered, hard hiking comes to the fore. The last boats to move into depower mode are fast. However, boats that fail to depower when overpowered are slow. Knowing when to make this transition is a key nuance to learn for your class. If you are light, hang on in here as your lightness will pay dividends downwind.

Helm inboard

Helm outboard

Upwind on Windy Days (Overpowered)

Hard work and depowering early is generally a fast combination on windy days.

Heel

Sailing the boat dead flat remains key. A touch of windward heel works well just before a big gust hits so that the gust drives you forward rather than causing heel. This is a key trick to sailing high and fast in these conditions as, by avoiding leeward heel, you avoid slipping to leeward as gusts hit. Every time your boat heels your foils lose depth in the water and you more readily get knocked sideways, especially in a gust. Furthermore, to stop the boat from spinning into the wind when you heel to leeward, you will need to pull your tiller to windward which generates a lot of drag and so is slow.

Sailing flat in breeze is much easier to say than do! Perfecting it comes from quality time on the water and being able to steer effectively with your head out of the boat, even when it is windy.

Trim

It can pay to sit back a little more, especially in waves and if sitting back moves you to a wider part of the boat. This change in position upwind is less than downwind. You might sit back by a backside's width but probably less than that and unlikely more than that. If your bow is persistently digging into waves it is probably time to sit back a little.

Rig Set Up

Ideally your rig should be set up so that, when fully hiked, your sails are sheeted in all the way in the lulls and spilling wind in the gusts. If you are always spilling wind you are creating a lot of drag from flogging sails, especially with a fully-battened mainsail. You need to know which levers to pull in your boat to depower (a Merlin Rocket is easy, an Enterprise hard). If your boat is hard to depower, it is better to sail flat with sails a fair way out than trying to hold on to too much power.

The cunningham is a very powerful aid for pulling draft forward to keep your sail shape, even as lots of kicker pulls draft aft. The cunningham

Even on windy days sailing the boat flat remains key

is also very effective at opening the upper leech. Dumping power high up is very useful because power high up has more heeling moment. Hard use of the cunningham with square top mains is very effective in breeze as a lot of drag can be eliminated by opening up the square head of the main.

Sail Trim

Working the mainsail hard is key. Playing the jib pays in some boats, though this is a trade-off as doing so can mean that the crew sits up from full hiking. Wind strength is constantly changing so your main should be on the move all of the time. In some boats it can pay to pinch in gusts as well as playing the main. The most powerful part of a gust is when it first hits, so pinching a touch just before it hits can gain you height, rather than gusts heeling you or blowing you sideways.

Body Positioning

Hard hikers tend to be fast in flat water and good steerers fast in waves. Being able to hike hard and steer well at the same time is definitely a skill worth working on. You should aim to hike near to straight-legged to protect your knees. Your upper body is then a powerful lever for responding to gusts or for full power hiking, i.e. straight legs and upper body level with the water. You should know your own fitness and for how long you can power hike. You should use hiking bursts at key times, for example to make a jump out the start, leebow a key opponent, win a tight finish, etc.

Power hike at key times

Centreboard

In some boats it is worth raising the centreboard, especially if you have raked the mast considerably. This can help balance up the rudder to reduce weather helm. This is more likely to pay in faster boats, especially if you can plane upwind (raising the board reduces drag).

Self-bailers

Typically sail with one down unless conditions are really rough and there is a lot of spray, when it is worth sailing with both down. You may have spent a few hours ensuring the bottom of your hull is smooth, so putting a self-bailer down should only be done when needed. Put your starboard bailer down first as it is less likely to leak when sailing slowly pre-start (which is generally done on starboard tack with leeward heel).

Upwind Differences between Single- & Double-handers

Body Movement & Positioning

Body movement in a single-hander is generally more effective as the boats are lighter, but it can still be highly effective in a double-hander if the helm and the crew can time their movements together.

Mainsheet Tension

Unstayed rigs, common in single-handers, typically have more mast bend and so have more luff curve cut into the sail. So your mast bend should match that luff curve, which is a compromise in all but medium winds. In light airs you might sheet in a little harder to match the two, avoiding an over-full luff entry and compromising by being near to stalling the leech. In windy weather you may choose not to sheet in too hard to avoid starving out the luff curve and having a very flat luff entry and diagonal creases radiating from the luff of the sail.

In double-handers, it is critical that the shape of your jib and mainsail match to prevent backwinding and to enable the air flow to move cleanly between the two.

Downwind Speed

Downwind you are always looking to go downhill on the biggest waves in the most wind!

Running in Single-handers

You should be looking for a path that keeps you heading down waves as much as possible. To do this you need to perfect staying on waves for as long as possible; moving quickly to the next wave; and searching for new waves.

To stay on a wave for as long as possible, you should aim down the wave and steer the angle that enables you to surf. Most single-handers have a flat spot on a dead run where the breeze struggles to create flow or reverse flow over the sail, so you should generally be steering around this spot; moving from sailing by the lee to sailing a broad reach, in rhythm with the waves and wind. Steering a dead run can occasionally pay if the direction of the waves enables that angle to give fast surfing.

To initiate surfing on a wave you need to pick up speed (generally by luffing) so that you are nearly at the same speed as the wave, and then pump and bear off as the wave hits the back of your boat. That pump can be aggressive as the rules limit the number of pumps but not how hard you pump. In lighter winds be careful not to pump too hard and backwind your sails. Timing is key because if your pump does not initiate surfing, your pump is illegal!

Once surfing a wave well, the trick to staying on it longer is being proactive about coming off the wave. Ideally, you should come off the wave and look for the next one before your 'ride' stops, i.e. before you stop planing and hit the bottom of the wave. However, exiting the wave too early means that you have missed some of the surf that you could have had on that wave. If the next waves don't look good, ride the wave you have for longer.

Waves are inconsistent in direction and size, so staying on the fastest downwind route means a lot of steering. If you are on a great wave you should generally stick with it even if it is taking you a long way off the rhumb line. If you are struggling to catch waves, you generally need to sail higher to pick up speed to get closer to the wave speed, which makes it easier to catch them. By taking big bear aways as you surf each wave, you have more scope to luff and increase speed to catch the next wave. If you get a good wave it often pays to almost forget where the mark is and surf the wave as long as possible before finding a new path to the mark. The biggest steerers downwind tend to be the fastest sailors.

It is rarely fast to let your main out past 90 degrees. It is quite hard to see where this point is from within the boat so it is good to mark this if you can, e.g. marking your mast when it is rotated 90 degrees versus a reference point on your mast collar or deck.

To sail fast downwind in any boat it is crucial to have clear water. It is very challenging to work waves effectively if they are confused and flattened by other boats' wakes. While it generally pays over a week to sail conservatively and tight into the fleet upwind, splitting often pays downwind as that crucially delivers clean waves.

Wave patterns differ every day so spend some time getting into the wave rhythm for that day. You should understand whether it is a day where your challenge is to catch the wave (generally the case with faster moving waves or lighter winds) or avoid sailing into the back of the next wave once you are surfing (generally the case with slower moving, choppier waves or more breeze). Get a feel for how consistent the waves are and what sort of angles feel fast before the race starts.

As with all of these changes in course, steering without using the rudder offers huge opportunities for gain.

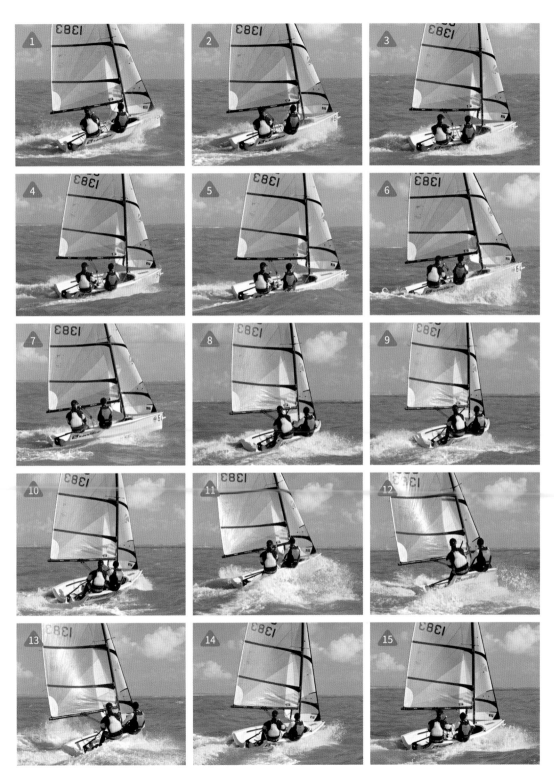

Lots of body steering is required to stay on the waves

Heel

There are potentially huge gains if you can use body movement to induce heel to steer, so keeping rudder movements to a minimum. So when you are luffing up to find the next wave you should be moving inboard. Move outboard to help your boat bear off. You will be turning a lot downwind with your rudder barely moving.

Trim

As well as sideways body movement to steer you also need to be moving fore and aft as your boat comes on and off the plane. Downwind sailing in marginal planing conditions is the point of sailing that requires the hardest work. As you come off the plane you need to slide forward to stop the flatter surfboard-shaped back of your boat sticking. As you get on the plane move aft to surf fast. How far you need to move depends on the hull shape of your class of boat, but most sailors do not move fore and aft enough.

Combining the fore-aft movement with sideways movement to body steer typically leads to a triangular-shaped movement. You should be moving out and back as you plane to bear off down a wave. As you sense you are about to come off the wave, move inboard to luff. When you are hunting the next wave you should move forward. As you catch the wave you should move outboard and aft to bear away and surf, and so the cycle goes. However, every wave is different and there are sometimes waves within waves so this pattern of movement is rarely uniform.

As for upwind, your body movement should reflect the sea state. If the waves are long and smooth, your body movement should match that; if the waves are short and choppy, your body movements should be short and punchy.

A good jury will not penalise you for this as all of your movement has a clear purpose – to sail your boat effectively over waves.

Use body movement to keep rudder movement to a minimum

Rig Set Up

If possible, rake your mast forward so it is upright. Some boats have raking rigs, and some classes allow you to remove some chocks from your mast gate so that your rig moves forward when you go downwind. Ease your outhaul to increase power, as your sail is still acting as an aerofoil on a run. If you have an inhaul, you should ease that rather than the outhaul to move the sail marginally higher up where there is more breeze. Set your kicker so that your upper leech is just opening and closing. You should have no cunningham and ensure that you have eased it before bearing off or you risk tearing your sail.

Sail Trim

You can also steer and reduce rudder use through sail trim. As you need to luff to find the next wave sheet in your main to help the boat luff. Ease your main as you bear off to help the boat do this with minimal rudder use. The speed of your sheeting should be varied according to how fast you need to steer. More steering is beneficial because you can justify harder, larger sail trims. You need to trim while keeping your tiller hand steady.

Steering through trimming rather than your rudder makes a big difference downwind as you should be doing a lot of steering.

Body Positioning

You should be sitting in a position that enables you to move quickly to adjust for wind and waves. Even in the lightest winds aim to have your backside just resting on the windward deck (and your legs pushing well to leeward to enable you do this). Sitting or crouching in the boat greatly reduces manoeuvrability which is so critical for steering downwind with minimal rudder action. By having your legs to leeward you can quickly bear off by moving them to windward without having to move your upper body.

Centreboard

Raise your centreboard as much as possible to reduce drag but without losing steerage. If you have too much centreboard up your boat will pitch from side to side as you steer. Aim to be on the edge of this state. This means that in light winds you can have more centreboard up than when it's windy.

Sailing in Pressure

Pressure is king on runs and generally more important than angles, unless the wind is very shifty.

Spotting pressure before others and sailing towards it is key. Being able to sail the boat down waves with effective body movement and trim is a hard skill to learn. The aim is to be able to do this and regularly glance backwards to map where the next pressure will be. This is harder to achieve than getting your head out of the boat upwind. However, with practice you will be able to do it quickly, rather than have to spend a lot of time looking backwards.

Body Movement

As for upwind, your body movement should match the size and frequency of the waves. So big waves require larger, more exaggerated, movements; long, smooth waves need smooth movements; choppy waves need punchier movements.

Your kinetics should be aggressive yet smooth. Your pumping should be hard with your sheet arm and steering smooth with your tiller arm. Both of these are difficult balances to achieve which is why sailing fast downhill isn't easy, but is hugely rewarding when perfected.

TOP TIP

Like picking windshifts, downwind sailing is an art rather than a science. Starts and boat handling are processes that can be broken down and perfected with focused time on the water. Picking shifts and sailing fast downwind can also be improved with practice but are harder to perfect and repeat. There is more feel and instinct to them. Your objective should be to keep improving so that, even on a bad day, you still pick shifts well because your head is out of the boat a lot, and you still sail well downwind because you can steer using little rudder. More time on the water and sailing against top notch shift pickers and fast downwind sailors definitely makes it easier to hit the shift and find your downwind 'rhythm'!

Picking shifts downwind is hard to perfect

Running in Two-sail Boats with No Spinnaker

There are a lot of similarities between running in two-sail boats without a spinnaker and single-handed sailing. Body movement and trim are still key.

The helm and crew should aim to move and trim in time, with the crew's range of movement typically bigger than the helm's. The crew does not have a tiller so can be much more mobile than the helm, which can add another dimension. A great crew is never static and has most of their weight on their feet / toes so that they are mobile downwind.

The angles steered cannot be as large as a single-hander because there are typically shrouds which prevent the main going out so far. However, having the main out against the boom and a relatively loose kicker can still create a sail shape than can be sailed effectively by the lee.

Variety of sailing can really help with this. Helms who have done some sailing in single-handers are usually more dynamic and fast downwind in two-man boats as the nuances of downwind body movement and trim are so critical in a single-hander.

Running with Symmetric Spinnakers

Similarities & Differences v. Single-handers

Again, there is a lot in common with single-handed sailing. Steering the waves aggressively using body movement and sail trim (with minimal rudder use) still pays massively. The biggest steerers who use the least rudder still tend to be fastest.

However, symmetric boats are the hardest in which to make this work, but consequently the most rewarding in terms of speed gain and satisfaction.

A symmetric spinnaker is easily collapsed with aggressive steering, so great helm-crew co-ordination is needed. It is hard for a crew to be mobile while handling a symmetric kite, but an agile crew who is putting most of his / her weight through their feet can still make it happen.

Angles

In some ways, symmetric running is similar to asymmetrics.

It generally pays to soak in light winds so that you are near to the point where you lose power completely (because there is no chance of planing by going high). This angle is of course much lower than can be achieved in an asymmetric.

It generally pays to head up (luff) to get planing early. In marginal planing, it generally pays to head up with the pole and spinnaker squared and steer to the windward kite luff.

When you are consistently planing, it generally pays to drop the pole and head up further. How much varies by boat.

The timing of these three transitions varies by class and wave state, and it is worth playing with in training and training events. Knowing how these grooves feel for each wind condition, and when to transition between them, is critical for consistent downwind speed.

Experiment to understand symmetric running transitions

Kite Setting

It can occasionally be worth letting the spinnaker collapse to get the best surf off a wave, which may mean nearly sailing by the lee or heading up faster than the spinnaker can move. It depends on the size of the waves and the gains possible.

It is important to arrive at the race course early to assess the waves and appropriate downwind steering for that day. Doing this with a tuning partner is ideal.

Reaching

Similarities & Differences v. Single-handers

The same principles apply as for single-handed sailing for body movement to steer in waves, when to come off them, and so on. However, the variation in angles should be smaller and steering smoother, as it would be impossible to keep the kite setting with some of the variation in angles that well-practised single-handed sailors perform. A good crew should be able to keep the spinnaker setting despite a lot of steering. This is very powerful as that then allows more steering and more distance to be gained from the waves. This takes a lot of practice and a crew with great feel.

Heel

In general, it pays to sail with a touch of leeward heel on reaches, especially in spinnaker boats because the spinnaker moves the centre of effort a long way forward. Raising some centreboard can balance the boat back up if that is an option.

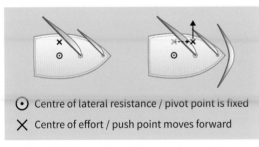

⊙ Centre of lateral resistance / pivot point is fixed

✕ Centre of effort / push point moves forward

Aim for a little leeward heel when reaching with a spinnaker

Rig Set Up

Set your rig up for maximum power (mast rake upright, outhaul eased, cunningham off) on reaches unless it is a tight reach and you are overpowered. Your kicker should be set using the same principles as running, with the kicker set so that the top of your leech is able to keep opening and closing. In pumping conditions you can sail with more kicker than this as your pump significantly opens the leech so you need more kicker to ensure you gain maximum drive from your pumping.

Sail Trim

Your sails should be constantly trimmed on a reach. You should be trimming to help you steer and also constantly trimming as the wind fluctuates in strength and direction.

Centreboard

Raise your centreboard to just before the point where you feel the boat slipping under you and you begin to lose steering. That will vary depending on the wind and wave state.

Asymmetric Sailing

Similarities & Differences v. Single-handers

The principles of body movement are very similar to single-handed sailing, but few double-handed sailors are dynamic enough downwind. Ease the spinnaker as much as possible so that the spinnaker luff is always on the edge of, or just, curling. Sailing the right angle downwind in asymmetrics is key.

You should experiment with different angles in training. The ideal is that you have multiple angles that work effectively in all conditions. You can then vary your angle, but keep your VMG (Velocity Made Good) to the next mark, depending on your tactical objectives at the time.

Experiment with different angles to maintain your VMG

Light Wind Angles

You should generally soak low in light winds (i.e. any wind state where there is no chance of planing). You should be sailing so low that the spinnaker is just on the edge of losing pressure in it. Helm-crew communication is vital in these conditions.

Soak lower than your opposition by:
- Sailing with a touch of windward heel.
- Having the spinnaker well eased so that the luff is generally just curling.
- Raising your centreboard a little.
- Possibly having the helm play the spinnaker sheet to have instant feedback between pressure in the spinnaker and steering. (This is not a good idea when racing among lots of boats as the helm needs to have their head out to make fast tactical decisions. If you do move into this mode, the crew should then be spotting pressure.)

You should also experiment to see if there is a higher mode in light winds where you sail a few degrees higher and have the spinnaker fully powering. Generally low gives the fastest VMG, but if you can find a high mode with the same, or nearly the same, VMG that opens up your tactical options nicely.

Windy Angles

When you are always planing downwind, most boats have a high and low planing mode. It varies by boat but some (like a Topper Xenon) like being sailed as low as possible while still just planing, whereas others (like a D-One) sail fast as high as you can go, with the kite on the edge of curling, to produce more apparent wind. Some asymmetrics (like an RS400) have both modes downwind, so then either mode can be used depending on where you are trying to position yourself for most breeze and where you want to be versus your competition.

A trick for gaining depth is to let your boat knock to leeward as gusts first hit. A light touch on the tiller, even when it is windy, will enable your boat to do that.

Marginal Planing Angles

These are some of the most enjoyable conditions downwind in an asymmetric. The first boat to go high and plane can make big gains. But it is a risky manoeuvre because, if you don't plane, you just sail extra distance for little gain. It helps to know your boat's downwind modes well and you should spend some time before the start understanding what sort of day it is. This can vary on each gybe, depending on the wave pattern, especially if there has been a recent windshift resulting in the waves being at an angle on one gybe but more square to you on the other gybe.

The first boat to go high and plane can make big gains

The Gybe Drop

This is a key manoeuvre to perfect in asymmetrics, as coming in on the inside at leeward marks with water on everyone on the opposite gybe is a powerful weapon for place gains. Being able to gybe drop as close to the mark as possible means that you can take more places by coming in on, or very close to, the layline at speed.

Coming in for a gybe drop at the leeward mark

Fixing an Attack of 'The Slows'

Everyone has occasions when they are not going as fast as they would like – the key is what you do about it.

In the Race

Fixing a dreaded dose of 'the slows' in a race is hard as there are so many variables and combinations of those which affect boatspeed. So a quick fix may not be easy.

But if you have put the quality time in, and know your boat, you should be confident that something odd is happening. In that case a few quick checks are worthwhile:

- Are you really going slowly or are you just in a lull? If you are sailing in a high quality fleet, you will probably spend ½ your time being 'slow' because the opposition have more wind than you.
- Are you tensing up because you feel slow and so are over-sheeting? Ease your sheets and relax your grip on the tiller. If possible, try placing your tiller extension to the side of you rather than in front of you to smooth out your steering. Gradually sheet back in as you feel yourself regaining the groove. This works most times.
- Talk to your crew for any insights.
- Look up at your rig and sails for anything obvious.
- Weed makes a huge difference. Raising your board mid-race can be costly. If you can heel to leeward and quickly glance at your foils you will lose less distance; so then you only need to raise the board or clear the rudder if necessary. Even a small bit of weed can upset the crucial flow over your foils. You should always do a weed check after the 5 minute warning signal.

- Check your settings – has a control line dropped out of a cleat?

If these approaches don't work, see if you can get a tuning partner, fast sailor or friend (ideally someone who is all three!) to have a look at your sailing between races.

Onshore

If you find that 'the slows' won't go away it is worth checking your boat over when you get ashore. Check to see whether anything has fundamentally changed in your boat. For example, is the mast straight? Has the slot gasket come away? Has the rigging stretched, changing your settings? And so on.

Check that the mast is straight if you are struggling to get rid of 'the slows'

If you are still stuck, talk to other sailors and see if they will have a look at your boat.

If you can, organise a RIB so that you can have a look from outside, or someone with a good eye can do the same. It is much easier to see what is fast or slow from outside a boat. Consider swapping boats with someone between races.

> *I have lost track of how many times I've had a dose of the dreaded slows! The most extreme were coming nearly last in races at two open meetings – an OK open in 1998 and a Merlin open in 2011. The OK 'slows' were down to a combination of factors including sheet tension, sail choice and being out of the groove, and so it took longer and quite a bit more experimentation to work out. In the Merlin, we were trying new things with rig tension settings at a training event. They clearly didn't work so we reverted back to our base settings.*

TOP TIP

Boatspeed is key. The old saying that boatspeed makes you look like a tactical genius is so true. Even a tiny boatspeed edge means that you will gain when you make ordinary tactical decisions, make big gains when you make right decisions and lose less when you make wrong ones.

Even World & National Champions have attacks of 'The Slows'!

Turning Corners

The key to boat handling is being able to steer the boat without slowing down.

How to Avoid the Handbrake (Rudder)

Changing direction with your rudder is slow. While the rudder is effective for steering, steering drags a piece of wood or carbon through the water at an angle which significantly slows your boat. Over a race, you will steer a huge amount, not just for boat handling manoeuvres but also steering through shifts upwind and waves downwind. Steering effectively makes a huge difference to speed around a race course. Often the fastest sailors are no quicker in a straight line, but they are much more effective at steering.

Boat handling is, in some ways, the easiest area of sailing to perfect because each manoeuvre is repeatable and relatively standard. With sufficient quality practice, your boat handling can be excellent. Pressure testing your boat handling is key. You can do this in training by doing a set number of tacks / gybes / spinnaker hoists / drops on a short course, rather than as leisurely manoeuvres. Doing this against another boat is a good way of seeing who has the better boat handling and learning from each other.

Heel

Steering through heel (windward heel to bear off, leeward to luff) will reduce your rudder use massively. It is worth practising with your tiller elasticated to the middle so that you learn how much heel your boat needs to steer in different conditions. You will need more heel to steer in light winds as your boat has less momentum. Sailing rudderless is widely recommended but changes the balance of your boat, so sailing with the rudder elasticated to the middle is more useful.

Sail Trim

Steer through sail trim in conjunction with heel. If you sheet in your main harder than your jib, you move the centre of effort back in the boat. Your pivot point (centre of your foils) does not change as you do this, so with the centre of effort moving behind your pivot point, your boat will naturally luff itself. If you sheet in your jib harder than your main, the reverse happens.

Tacking

You should be using as little rudder as possible in a tack. A good technique to dampen rudder use is to take your tiller extension round the back of the boat rather than in front of you. This tends to lead to a smaller and smoother movement.

To initiate the turn you should heel slightly to leeward and pull in the main a couple of clicks on the ratchet. By doing this, your rudder should largely move by itself without having to be pushed much. You shouldn't have to move the rudder past half way over. Do not use too much leeward heel going into the tack or you will slip sideways.

Light Winds

Boat handling in light winds is especially important as the difference between a good and bad tack or gybe is at its greatest.

Most sailors start their roll too early in light winds. In general, your roll shouldn't start until you are around head to wind. If you roll too early, your boat will try to bear off and you will need to use more rudder to turn which has a strong handbrake effect. By rolling later you have less time for the roll and for flattening out the roll at the end of the tack. As the time for those actions is condensed, they can be more aggressive. Ideally, your movement should be aggressive but very smooth.

You may need a little more kicker on during the

Tack using as little rudder as possible

tack to ensure that your main drives out the tack to avoid air disappearing out the top of an open leech.

Your roll should be as hard as you can so that you are just on the edge of not being able to move back against it. It typically pays to roll as much as you can without shipping water, but be mindful of Rule 42.

Fitness and agility can help even in the lightest of winds.

Moderate Winds

Your tack in moderate winds should be similar in shape to a light wind roll tack, but you will need less exaggerated body movement and even less rudder to achieve the same effect.

Windy Conditions

When it's windy you may choose to move to 'safety tacks'. At training events do this as late as possible and push up the range in which you can tack normally. A safety tack means no roll (or as little roll as possible) in the tack. You'll need a harder turn on the rudder to ensure that you don't get stuck in irons (which is a high risk place to be when it's windy, due to both capsize risk and loss of control with other boats around moving fast). Ensure that you ease some main as you go into the tack so that you are safe on your exit from the tack. A faster turn on the tack is possible as you aren't going through the movements to ensure a good roll tack.

Waves

In waves you should generally use less roll as you are more likely to ship water. If tactical considerations allow, tack in a flatter spot of water so that you can use more roll and have a more effective tack. Aim to tack on the top of the wave so that you have a chance of completing the tack before the next wave hits. If it is choppy this may be impossible to pull off so ensure that your rig is set up for acceleration at the exit of the tack, i.e. more open leeches via less sheet tension / kicker and a touch of leeward heel to ensure the foils are still biting at lower speed.

Gybing

Light Winds (opposite)

In light winds your boat does not have much momentum. You should move pretty sharply to windward to initiate the turn, to avoid having to use the rudder to do this. In general you should roll as much as possible, so be just on the edge of shipping water or the boom hitting the water. As you bring the boat upright out of the gybe be careful not to knock the wind out of the sails if the wind is very light. If that does happen, gently ease your sails back out to avoid them backwinding and decelerating you. Again be mindful of Rule 42.

Moderate Winds

In moderate winds, the initial movement to turn the boat does not need to be as marked. The sequence of moves is the same as those for light winds, but again with less exaggerated body movement.

Windy Conditions (overleaf)

You should aim to gybe when your boat is accelerating or at maximum speed as that reduces the apparent wind so making the gybe easier. Time your gybe for when you are just starting to sail down a wave, or just after a gust has first hit, so that you are accelerating. This also gives you more time to gybe before you potentially decelerate due to sailing into the back of the next wave or the gust running out.

Aim for no roll on the gybe, which often means crossing the boat just before the sails have gybed. Release some kicker before the gybe to depower the mainsail as you exit the gybe. Veer towards over- rather than under-steering because, if it doesn't work out, a leeward capsize is faster to recover from than a windward one.

Swinging the boom to initiate the mainsail going through the gybe can help to prevent the boom moving over very quickly, which makes the boat harder to control. Aim to swing the boom when the main is at its lightest so that the impact of it hitting the new side is least, giving you the best chance of staying dry. Practice will help you know at what point in the gybe the main is at its lightest.

A key point for surviving a windy gybe is your exit angle. Typically there is a safe angle where you won't capsize to windward as you aren't too high, nor will you capsize to leeward as you aren't too low. Learning this angle for your boat comes through practice and focusing on your exit angle as you go through the gybe.

Practice, and a lot of swimming, makes for perfect windy gybes! This is a great thing to practise outside of racing, ideally in more wind than you would normally gybe in during a race, and somewhere warm (Lake Garda is perfect for this!). Outside of racing there is no cost to capsizing (other than getting wet!) so you should practise really fast gybes. This will give you a feel for how fast you can steer and move across the boat through gybes before you need to slow them down to stay upright.

If your sailing programme does not allow you the time for practice outside of racing then you should seek to move your windy gybing on at training events, even if that means capsizing occasionally.

720s

The main question is whether you should tack or gybe first.

If you are sailing upwind, initiate your 720 with a tack. If that tack is well executed, the penalty is effectively a 630. Likewise, downwind you should initiate your 720 with a gybe. Remember, as always, it is best to try to do the turns without using much rudder.

> **TOP TIP**
>
> **Good boat handling requires a lot of body movement to avoid rudder use. Being able to move dynamically without moving the tiller around is a key skill.**

In light winds use roll to help you gybe

In strong winds use much less roll, crossing the boat just before the sails have gybed

Many places can be won or lost when rounding marks.

The Windward Mark

Approach

Even before the race starts you should have a plan for your windward mark approach. That plan may change but at least you have a plan! If you think high will pay on the first reach, or you plan a straight set for an asymmetric run, you want to be high of the pack coming into the windward mark so that you can go high on the next leg. If you think low will pay on the reach, or plan a gybe set in an asymmetric, you can push down more onto the layline.

Plan your approach to the windward mark

Rounding

As with all boat handling, you should use as little rudder as possible. So ease the main faster than the jib and use windward heel to bear away. You will generate turning momentum which you will need to reverse to stop bearing away – use some leeward heel and sheet in the main to stop the turn rather than pushing your rudder.

After the Mark

It is now time to execute your plan. In general, half measures don't work on reaches. You either need to go high in clear wind and water or sufficiently low to also sail in clear wind and water. Remember, this positioning is just versus the boats that can disturb your wind and water. So you could have half the fleet higher than you and half lower but if you are clearly high or low of the boats around you, you are in a clear wind and wave lane.

In general, a high route pays on a tight reach and a lower route on a broad reach. You should have a good reason to deviate from these golden rules, but ensuring clear wind / water can be such a reason.

The Gybe Mark

Approach

The earlier you form a plan for the gybe mark, the better your chances of a good rounding. You should have a 'plan A' before the start: e.g. if you see that the second reach is tight you are probably going to want to be high on it and so need an inside overlap to execute that. If the second reach is very broad you may well go low and so an inside overlap is less critical and is unlikely to be something you would sacrifice distance for.

If you are in a pack of boats on the first reach you should be looking very early for a route to either gain an inside overlap or break clear so that you round with no one inside you. This needs to be an early decision. Indecision often leads to being caught outside a pack, which is especially costly if the next reach is a tight one.

Rounding

Aim for a nice smooth turn: a little like the way a motor racing driver takes the apex of a corner. Again you should use heel and sail trim to minimise rudder use.

Aim for a nice smooth turn at the gybe mark

After the Mark

Your route after the mark depends on how tight the reach is, where pressure is and where the other boats are. If you are in a pack, it generally pays to find clear air by going high. A low route can pay if the fleet is luffing each other high, especially when there is tide pushing the fleet upwind. A high route pays more often on the second reach than the first reach because the inside overlap at the next mark is to windward on the second reach whereas it is to leeward on the first reach.

You should have your post-mark plan in mind before you approach the gybe.

The Leeward Mark

Approach

Again, the earlier you form a plan for your leeward mark rounding, the better chance you have of executing it well. Form a 'plan A' before the start. If you think left will pay upwind you will be looking for an early tack. This is easier to execute from an inside overlap so you may choose to sacrifice distance to achieve it. If you think right will pay, you are looking for a great lane out of the leeward mark.

If there are two leeward marks, spend some time before the start working out which leeward mark is further upwind, and by how much, as this will have a major impact on your downwind route decisions.

Rounding

Again, you should avoid using the rudder as much as possible. Leeward heel and a faster sheet-in of the main than the jib will help you to head up. Exaggerate this in light winds, when your boat has less momentum.

After the Mark

Your key priority is to establish a clear lane quickly in the direction that you would like to go. Often that means sailing free, high or tacking to establish that lane.

Establish a clear lane quickly after the leeward mark

CHAMPIONSHIP

SAILING

PART 4

Sailing at Championships

As I have already said, sailing is a very complex sport. At training events, you should try to keep dissecting the sport, experimenting with new ideas, learning, putting your processes back together and then breaking them up again.

At big events you should keep it simple. Stop trying new things and sail instinctively. Most big events are won or lost before the event, so what you have learnt through the season will now show through. It is too late to change anything now, so this is the time to enjoy putting everything together and sail at your best without the distraction of training objectives!

By trying new things at the smaller events, the big events are in many ways easier, which is a nice mindset with which to go into a championship.

The best practice to get good at big fleet sailing is, unsurprisingly, big fleet sailing! Experienced big fleet sailors are able to glance around quickly and understand immediately where they are versus the fleet, understand how much risk they are taking and assess that against their objectives. This sounds complex but with experience it becomes almost instinctive, so the sailor is focused on speed rather than having to look around at the fleet too much.

While a little tedious, checklists can be useful at big events as it is easy to forget something critical (e.g. food, the most important thing!). A checklist should include all the things you need, e.g. multitool, tape, spares, food, water, etc.

Being able to start well in big fleets is a key skill

Key Skills

Big Fleet Starts

Being able to start consistently well in big fleets is a key skill for delivering a successful championship series. Starting (covered in more detail in the next chapter) is a process, albeit a relatively complex one. Like any process it can be perfected if each part of it is well practised. It is easier to perfect starting than picking shifts or sailing fast downwind, which are more of an art.

Risk Management

You should have a clear outcome objective for your event before you go into it. However, at the regatta, focus on process objectives rather than your outcome objective because the outcome of the event is not in your control and therefore focusing on that alone can lead to frustration and a worse performance. You can sail a brilliant week but someone else may be on fire. Your goals should be focused on what you can control: sailing the right course and not forgetting anything each day (such as your tally). You can't control whether you hit the groove of the waves and shifts that week or how well your opposition does.

So coming 50ᵗʰ in an event can be a great result if you've hit all of your process objectives, whereas you might not be wholly happy if you've missed your process objectives but won.

This approach is a great way to de-pressurise and de-stress events.

Having said all that, half of your brain still needs to be focused on your outcome objective. This is a hard mental exercise to pull off. It is around your outcome objective that you should manage risk:

- If you are behind your outcome objective you should increase risk. Go for more punchy starts, sail harder to the side of the course that you think is paying, push your boat handling harder, edge towards more 50/50 boat-on-boat situations.
- If you are ahead of your outcome objective you should be more conservative. However, backing down too much on starts will lead straight away to a poor start. So it generally

works to still start pretty hard but stay with the fleet strategically, be highly conservative with the rules and take some more time on boat handling, especially if it's windy.

> **"** *It is good to have an idea of where you are versus your outcome objective even before an event starts. We went into the 2008 Endeavour Trophy with a very light wind forecast and were a few stone heavier than some of the potential contenders. Our outcome objective was to win. We knew that if we started reasonably well we might just make the top 5. So we aimed to win every start pushing the line and ends hard. This strategy carried a high risk of multiple OCSs in an 8 race, 1 discard series. But it gave us a crack at winning and we were solely focused on that outcome objective. We just got away with the starts and won overall.* **"**

Sailing the Fleet

Managing risk is about where you are versus the fleet, not where you are versus the course. You could be in the middle of the course but, if most of the fleet is one side of you, you are taking a risk (which may or may not be appropriate in that race). You should always have an idea where you are versus the fleet. This is an important role for a top crew.

Cover the fleet if you are leading

With plenty of big fleet experience, where you are versus the fleet becomes instinctive, so you can spend minimal time looking for this and focus on boatspeed and windshifts. With a drilled-in risk-averse approach you should feel uncomfortable as soon as you start splitting from the fleet and be looking for the first shift / gust back to consolidate, unless your clear plan for that race is to gamble.

Strategy

The foundation for consistent big fleet results is having a race plan based on as much information as possible.

Attitude to Risk

Your attitude to risk in each race depends on whether you are ahead of or behind your outcome objective. If you are ahead, you should sail more conservatively. This low risk approach typically helps deliver a consistent series. However, if you are single-mindedly focused on your outcome objective you should increase risk to try to hit it.

So you will typically start a week low risk. And hopefully end it low risk! If you can stay low risk, others will have to increase their risk and probably rack up points. But if you are behind your objective, it may be very appropriate to, for example, hit a corner in the last race to try to claw back points to hit your goal.

There are times when a low risk strategy can be counterproductive. Trying to sail low risk in very unstable winds, or when you are ahead in any asymmetric boat downwind, can result in you being sucked backwards as you become reactive to shifts and breeze whilst your competitors are being proactive. In these circumstances it pays to still attack the shifts and gusts, but keep half an eye on where your competition is and try to stay on the same part of the course as them whilst attacking

the shifts and gusts on the way there. Not easy!

Course Bias

This is the most important factor in deciding which way to go up the first beat. You should aim to have your bow out (ahead of most of the fleet) on the long tack, then you will gain most of the time. So if the first beat is starboard tack biased, you will be looking to get to the left of the fleet so that you gain from any header. As you are on starboard for most of the beat, time is on your side and at some point a header will come for you to profit from. You will be unlucky (or have not tracked the breeze well) for the breeze to only unexpectedly lift up the beat, causing you to lose out. And vice versa for a port tack biased beat.

By always aiming to have your bow out on the long tack, the odds are stacked in favour of the shifts going your way, which greatly helps deliver big fleet consistency. You should have a good reason not to have your bow out on the long tack.

When you are unsure of what is happening strategically, sticking to this simple rule generally works.

Wind Pattern

You should track the wind for as much as an hour before the start to understand the shift pattern. Practice beats can help with this. Reviewing some weather forecasts to understand where the next shift may come from can help, although weather

forecasts tend to be over quite a long period. You should understand the impact of land and clouds on the breeze, whether it is an unstable or stable breeze and what a sea breeze may do. This is a big topic that is covered in *Wind Strategy* by David Houghton and Fiona Campbell.

In light winds there is often more breeze at the edge of the course where it isn't so disturbed by the fleet, so sailing the corners more is sometimes required. Pressure is a much more important factor in light winds as a few knots more wind will make a big difference to both your speed and height. However, a few knots more wind when it is windy makes little difference to speed and height.

Tide

Prior knowledge of a venue, either through your own experience or talking to people, is the most valuable information you can have. Tidal charts can be useful but may not be subtle or detailed enough to provide the insights that you need for short course dinghy sailing. You can often find information on the day by observing where shallow water may be, looking for tide lines and seeing who gains when splitting tacks with a tuning partner before the start.

Land Influence

It is rare that the land does not have a major influence on the wind. Many books have been written about this so justice can't be done to the subject here! As well as land impact on wind bends and convergence, you should consider the impact on the stability of the breeze. Offshore winds tend to be more unstable which moves your strategy towards taking shifts up the middle of the course.

Waves

There are sometimes significantly more waves or choppier water on one part of the course, which may lead you to avoid that part of the beat. Choppy water may also indicate shallow water or a tide line, which may be useful information for your tidal strategy.

The Plan

Based on these six factors, you should form an idea of which way you think it will pay to go up the beat. It is critical to be honest with yourself. Being unsure is absolutely fine and pretty common. That, in itself, is powerful information as you can then manage risk effectively and stick to the middle of the fleet. Only taking a side of the fleet when you are very sure, and sailing the middle when you're not, is one of the magic ingredients of the holy grail of big fleet consistency.

You should also talk to people who have sailed at your regatta venue before the event to see if they have any insights. Use any information available online and dig into your venue notes – you should keep a record of what works at different venues for future reference.

Starts at Championships

Starts are less important in smaller fleets and shiftier winds, so the ability to start consistently well is a key skill in the transition from leading club racer to championship sailor.

Slow Speed Boat Handling

Slow speed boat handling is the foundation for strong starting. It is a distinct skill: sailors can be fantastic at normal speed boat handling but still weak at slow speed boat handling. However, it is an area few sailors practise. Being able to handle your boat effectively at slow speeds will enable you to generate space quickly on a start line, thus reducing the time for anyone else to fill that critical space.

Boats behave very differently at fast and slow speeds. At slow speeds the foils are starting to stall or are completely stalling, so the boat becomes a very different beast.

Stalling Foils

As your boat slows, the flow over your foils will eventually stall. Your boat then behaves totally differently. The key is to practise sailing your boat with both stalled foils and foils on the edge of stalling. You need to learn where that knife edge is for your boat in all conditions. You should aim to stay on the knife edge of stalling foils better than your competition. By doing that you can crucially creep towards the line more slowly than other boats in the last minute before the start and give yourself more space to accelerate.

You should also practise generating a gap to leeward as quickly as possible by being able to sail your boat up to and just beyond head to wind without losing control. While you have no rights if you go beyond head to wind, you can briefly do this as long as you don't infringe other boats, thus gaining more space to leeward. So being able to steer some big angles and manage that with aggressive but legal rudder use, heel and sail trim is a key skill. The combination of those three weapons varies by boat but can be effectively learnt with practice.

A quick double tack is also a powerful tool to have in your starting armoury. If space develops to windward, a double tack can quickly deliver a leeward gap and is an easier and faster manoeuvre than holding your boat around head to wind to generate leeward space.

In general, you need leeward heel to keep your foils biting longer. In lighter winds, this generally means standing up rather than sitting comfortably on the sidedeck!

Also, you should practise controlling your boat with stalled foils. Then if you do accidentally (or need to) slow down so that your foils stall, you can remain in control.

Generating space on a start line needs slow speed boat handling skills

Exercises

An effective exercise for learning about your boat's stalling foils is stopping by a mark and aiming to stay within around a boat's length of it for two minutes. You should vary this one boat's length gap depending on how easy your boat is to handle at low speeds, what the wind strength is and how experienced you are at this. Line up next to the buoy to simulate both a starboard- and port-biased start line.

As part of this exercise, aim to be at full speed right by the mark on the start gun. Being able to bring your boat up to speed, known as 'pulling the trigger', in as short a space of time and water as possible is a key skill in a crowded start.

This isn't the most exciting exercise, so trying this little but often works well. Do this two or three times before racing every time you sail and you will quickly develop great slow speed boat handling skills.

The Start Process

1 Hour to 10 Minutes Pre-start

This is a key time because your information gathering during this period will determine your chances of getting the first beat right. Your starting strategy is closely linked to your first beat plan so this information is doubly important. The table below shows the 9 start scenarios:

	Start line bias	Pre-race analysis	Starting strategy
1	Starboard	Go right	Start on, or very near to, the committee boat so that you can tack early and get your bow out on the tack towards the favoured side. This is a high risk start so should be considered in the context of your risk management for that race.
2	Starboard	Go up the middle	Start near the committee boat to take advantage of the bias but look for space so that you can quickly drive over the fleet on starboard tack to get into the middle of the course.
3	Starboard	Go left	Similar to start 2 but space to leeward out of the start is everything as you will have to live with the lane you create on starboard tack for some time.
4	Unbiased	Go right	Depending on how strongly you think right will pay, and your attitude to risk for that race, start towards, or even right next to, the committee boat.
5	Unbiased	Go up the middle	Start around the middle of the fleet (not necessarily the middle of the line) in as much space as you can to give early room to tack, thus providing flexibility in your route decisions.
6	Unbiased	Go left	Depending on how strongly you think left will pay, and your attitude to risk for that race, start towards, or even right next to, the pin end.
7	Port	Go right	Start towards the pin end to take advantage of the line bias. Seek to create a gap in front / leeward of yourself in the pre-start and use up all of the leeward gap in the last seconds before the start to create room to tack early.
8	Port	Go up the middle	Same as start 7, as you are looking for an early tack.
9	Port	Go left	Start near, or even on, the pin end. A gap to leeward is key as you will have to live with the lane you create out of the start for some time. Starting right on the pin is high risk but guarantees a great lane if you pull off a winning pin end start.

You should overlay your attitude to risk for the race, backing away from the ends or crowds if you are looking for a low risk race. Note that starting at the ends is especially high risk because, if you get it wrong, you can hit the end or miss it, whereas the cost of a poor start away from the ends is usually less.

You should also know your boat and your capability in it. Some boats handle better in tight situations, and pre-start boat handling requires practice. So if you are new to a boat, or rusty, you may back-off from tight spots and vice versa.

In very light winds it often pays to start at the ends, especially in big fleets. The wind has little energy so dirty air and the deflection of wind as it passes over the fleet is bigger mid-line, leaving light and disturbed wind there.

You need to practise all of these types of starts in your training events to become comfortable with every type of start. You will know which of these starting types you relish and which you approach with slight trepidation. You should put yourself out of your comfort zone at training events, challenging yourself to pull off great starts in your weaker areas. Also start in the pack at training events to improve your ability to pull off the really tough starts. It is rare that there is lots of space in a big fleet start, so by pushing yourself to start in the pack at smaller events you can simulate big fleet starts all year round rather than just once or a few times a year, massively accelerating your learning curve.

10 Minutes to 5 Minutes Pre-start

Once you have gathered all of your information about the race course for that day, it is time to check transits and line bias. While doing this, you should remain aware of anything that may change your first beat plan, especially the windshift and gust pattern.

It is rare that there is a perfect transit on the shore in line with the start line. If not, this should not be a concern. You should aim to have two or three transits at either end of the line. Ideally, one for when you are over the line, one on and one behind. And, if you can, get a picture of what you see in between them. This typically means having a look a few times so that you can form a map of the start line geography in your head, at both ends if possible. In the reality of a crowded start line, it is rare that you can see your on line transit, but just a glimpse of what you can recall on the landscape can give you the confidence to take a crucial jump on the fleet.

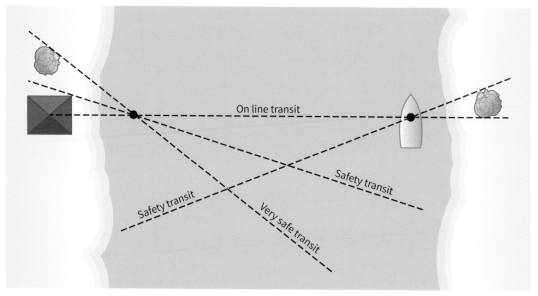

Getting transits

If there are no transits, this is a great opportunity for a flying start! No one else will have a transit so there is typically a lot of line sag giving you the chance to make a jump on the fleet away from the ends if that fits with your first beat plan. There is typically more line sag on longer start lines, with lower quality fleets and where there is more adverse tide and wind or waves.

There are several methods of checking line bias. My preferred one is to sail in one direction along the start line, set the sails and cleat them. You should use your transits to ensure that you are sailing exactly along the start line. Then sail the other way along the start line leaving your sails cleated or keeping them in the same position. If you have to sheet in to trim the sails you are sailing a more upwind angle so sailing towards the biased end. Once you have transits, this method is quick and so can be repeated several times. I find it the most accurate method as it can pick up on small amounts of line bias.

> **TOP TIP**
>
> Start your watch for the 5 minute gun or synchronise it for the 4 minute gun right next to the committee boat, ideally listening to anyone counting down the time on the committee boat. The speed of sound is around 340 metres per second, so you can easily lose ½ second or more if you start your watch away from the committee boat. In a competitive big fleet, this can be the difference between a great and ordinary start.
>
> Also, wear your watch on your right wrist or place it on the mast if that works in your boat so you are looking forwards when looking at your watch.

5 Minutes to 1 Minute (or sooner depending on the boat) Pre-start

During this period you should keep your head out of the boat and be aware of any changes in wind across the course, or signs of change from the clouds, and consider the impact of this on your starting plan – both in terms of line bias and which way may pay up the first beat.

As you move towards one minute (or sooner with a densely populated start line), you should find space in the area that you would like to start. Remain flexible. For example, if the line is starboard-biased but you want a low risk start, that generally means starting away from the committee boat. However, if everyone is doing that, there can be lots of room at the committee boat. That often happens early in a series when most boats are looking to de-risk their starts.

Starting in as much space as possible reduces the cost of a sub-standard start. With fewer boats around you there is much more likely to be room to tack or sail free and find a lane than if you are starting in a pack.

Choosing who you line up near is very important. Ideally you should line up near boats you know you can outpace. That gives you a strong chance of gaining a crucial early lane and also enables you to start worry-free. By the same token, it is very powerful to gain a reputation for being fast and difficult to start near. This is worth cultivating at training events.

The Final Minute Pre-start

You should be seeking to line up bow down (i.e. slightly behind) on the boats around you. This ensures that you won't be black-flagged or put your sail number in the race officer's head. You should just have your bow overlapping with the front row so you keep your 'starting slot'. This gives you more space to accelerate into, so that you can sheet in before everyone else and hit the start line with more speed. Lining up bow down also means that you don't give away where your transits are.

You should reveal your transit as late as possible. So, ideally, you should accelerate and sheet in once and not slow down again, using every inch of your transit – hitting your on line transit just as the start gun goes. Judging time and distance is key for this. Spending some time pre-start understanding your speed of travel against your transits can be a helpful exercise, especially in tide.

This is potentially a risky starting strategy because if you don't sheet in first when lining up bow down, you will be rolled. You need confidence in your transits and the time and distance it will take to sail to those transits. If you are 100% confident of both, anyone who sheets in before you will be OCS, so it is unlikely that anyone will do that. If you are not fully confident in your transits or time to the start line, you should line up further forward on the boats around you.

Create space to leeward as late as possible to reduce the risk of that lovely gap being filled by a latecomer. Being able to create that gap quickly is a key benefit of practising your slow speed boat handling. With a **starboard-biased start line** you are looking for a gap to leeward, as it is going to take some time to get your bow forward and have room to tack. So you are going to have to live with the lane you created pre-start for some time – therefore a gap to leeward is key.

In the last minute you need to be highly aware of boats potentially coming in and filling your gap to leeward. In a two-man boat the helm's sight should be more focused to leeward as you need a fast reaction to stop a boat filling your gap there. The crew should then be more focused on looking to windward for transits and cover, i.e. are other boats covering your sail numbers from the race officer's view?

To prevent someone coming in to leeward you need to fill the gap before they arrive. By doing this they will generally be put off and seek an easier gap. You should fill the gap by bearing off hard so that your boat spins 90 degrees to fill the gap as much as possible. You should bear off 'badly' so that you move forward as little as possible and use as little of your hard-earned gap to leeward as possible. A bad bear off involves using lots of rudder so that your boat turns but doesn't accelerate, which preserves as much of your gap to leeward as possible. Use heel and sails to fight the turn, i.e. use more rudder, leeward heel and sheet the main in while easing the jib. As soon as the potential boat filling your gap has headed on their way, you should luff back up hard and use the

momentum from your bear off to claw back some distance to windward via luffing back up beyond head to wind (without infringing other boats) to re-open your gap to leeward. If there is space, a quick double tack is highly effective at re-establishing your leeward gap. All of these moves need practise in training time.

If you find yourself in a pile-up, or even just a crowd, from which a good start looks challenging, be quick to escape and find space if you see that there is more space elsewhere.

With a **port-biased line** you are generally looking to tack early to consolidate a (hopefully) strong start. To do this, a gap to *windward* is needed. So create a gap to leeward in the pre-start period and then sheet in really early to use up that gap and create a gap to windward on the start gun which will give you the room to tack early. If you don't envisage that you will be able to tack quickly, you will also need to leave some gap to leeward so that you have a lane out of the start. This is a very hard start to pull off, but very rewarding as not many boats will manage it.

> ## TOP TIP
>
> You can typically sheet in earlier on a port-biased line because that bias means that you are at a lower angle on starboard tack to the start line so take longer to cross it. This also means that there is typically more line sag on a port-biased line. If you can make room to be one of the first to tack out, you are probably laughing your way to at least a top five placing at the windward mark!

As you accelerate for the start to (ideally) hit the line at full speed on the start gun, ensure that you use heel and sail trim to accelerate so that you accelerate faster than other boats around you. Your initial bear off to accelerate should be initiated with windward heel and early jib trim, then straighten your course and luff with leeward heel and fast main trimming.

There is a lot going on during this last minute but you also need to keep your head out of the boat and stay observant, especially in shifty, unstable breezes. You may need to change your plan quickly and move up or down the line if you see new pressure or a shift coming. This is a key role of a top crew.

Review how often you are OCS. If it is rare, you should be pushing your starts harder.

The First Minute

Gains in the first minute of the race are massively magnified as you go through the race because the early leaders benefit from clear air, clear water and control of their race plan. So it is key to hike at your absolute hardest as soon as there is wind for at least the first minute or until you poke your bow out from the pack. Sprint hiking and trimming hard for 10 seconds can work to get your nose out. Sprint hiking is where you hike to your absolute maximum for a burst and then rest up a little to get the blood back through your legs. In light winds all the smooth steering and movement you have practised should give you the confidence to relax and sail fast.

In this first minute, you should drive home your first beat strategy. If your plan is to get left, sail a little lower than usual if there is space. If you are unsure which way will pay and find you are to the left of the fleet, sail a bit higher or tack on the next small shift / gust. You should sail low or high using your rig set up and heel (a touch of leeward heel to sail high, dead flat to sail low) rather than dragging your rudder around If you are looking to head right, you should tack early or proactively find a lane to tack by sailing high to force the boats above you to tack or, if your start was not so strong, look for a gap to tack and duck transoms.

Recovery from Poor Starts

Unless you are a starting god, your starts will occasionally go wrong. So the ultimate big fleet sailing weapon is being able to recover from a poor start or first shift.

Revisit Strategy

With everything happening fast, it is often time to trust your instincts. Instincts are developed from your past experiences so are often right in the heat of the battle when you have little time to rethink your plan.

If you have time, get your head out of the boat and look for any factors that may change your strategy. You should seek to be back on strategy as soon as you can.

Clean Air

If you have a poor start you may be a couple of lengths behind the leaders at that point. If you can get to the top mark still only a couple of lengths behind the leaders you will certainly be in the top five! Losses at the start are greatly magnified by sailing in dirty air.

Dirty air is a killer because the wind is slowed but, more importantly, confused; it is near impossible to have your rig working efficiently when sailing in dirt. The most dirty air and water is at the start as the fleet is at its most compact. Finding clear wind is challenging in a big fleet after a poor start. You are looking to find as good lanes of clear wind as possible, while still going the right way according to your first beat game plan (or revised plan if you have seen something change).

If you are forced to sail in dirty air, adapt your dynamic settings so that your rig copes more effectively. Dirty air is confused in direction and strength. Use less mainsheet and kicker so that your sails can breathe better and you have more acceleration as dirty air slows you. A touch of leeward heel and sailing slightly freer can help to keep your foils biting through dirty water.

Holding Lanes

It is key to know what a 'lane' of clear air looks like for your class of boat and how you sail. Some boats can sail well in a leebow position, others can't. Where the dirty wind sits to leeward of another boat's sails varies by boat. Understanding these two things is key to understanding where the lanes may be for your boat.

Two-boat tuning and putting yourself under pressure at training events is key to being able to sail in 'narrow lanes' rather than 'fat lanes'. In two-boat tuning you should practise sailing in difficult positions. That will narrow the lanes you are able to hold. The narrower the lane you can still sail in reasonably fast will dramatically improve your chances of finding a lane that keeps you on your first beat game plan. This is the key reason why some sailors can seemingly always recover from a poor start. They can sail in a narrower lane so spend less time being bounced from tack to tack

and can quickly get back on their race plan.

You can sail for longer in a tight spot using your settings and heel. So, if you are in danger of being leebowed, move into 'high' mode with tighter leeches and a touch of leeward heel. Do the opposite to sail free if you are in danger of being rolled. You can also use these techniques for sailing higher or lower to expand your lane. It is worth proactively expanding your lane even if you feel comfortable in it. A header can quickly cause a leeward boat to potentially leebow you, or a lift can give a windward boat the opportunity to potentially drive over the top of you. So proactive lane expansion is a powerful weapon.

Lanes are more important in steady wind and one-sided courses because you will have to live with the lane you pick. In very shifty winds finding a lane doesn't really matter. So finding, expanding and keeping lanes is a key skill in the transition from a good lake sailor to a sea / big fleet sailor.

In light winds, the wind is more disturbed by packs of boats as the wind has less energy. So you can make gains by avoiding packs of boats and trying to get in anti-phase on the shifts / gusts versus packs of boats that form.

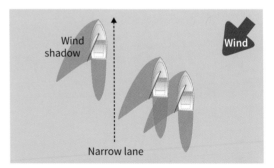

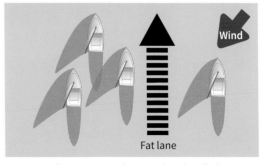

Practise sailing in narrow lanes rather than fat lanes

Chip Away v. Corners

In general it pays to chip places away after a poor start by finding lanes whilst staying on strategy. However, hitting a corner usually delivers clean air so it can be a better plan than sailing in the middle of the pack with dirty wind and confused waters. So if you can't find any lanes, corners are generally preferable.

Hitting a corner is high risk as even a small shift can lose you a lot of places. Or gain them! So in some circumstances a corner is appropriate. If you need a top five position in the last race of an event to achieve your outcome objective, and chipping away is unlikely to get you there, hitting a corner is a smart plan.

Starting early in a gate start can be a risky strategy

Gate Starts

When to Start

When you start should be assessed versus the fleet's position, not distance along the gate. So a start 2 minutes into a 4 minute gate is early if most of the fleet start late, and vice versa.

A good conservative strategy is to start towards the middle of the pack. More boats are able to execute a good start on a gate start, whereas a good start is harder to achieve on a line start. So it generally takes longer to find space to tack after a gate start. Hence any leverage (i.e. distance between you and the middle of the fleet) at the start gun is magnified as you will probably be unable to tack for some time. Also a gate start is dynamic whereas a line start is fixed, so leverage versus the fleet is also magnified by the moving nature of a gate line.

Gate start lines are also typically much longer than a fixed line start. So starting to one side of the fleet is a much higher risk strategy for a gate start. That risk can be appropriate depending on where you are relative to your objectives and how confident you are in which side of the beat will pay.

If you are slower than the fleet in the conditions of that day, it generally pays to start later. If you start early, and you are slow, you are likely to get spat out and have to sail in horrible dirty air and water for longer. If you are fast, an early start would seem logical but remains high risk. It is rare that a boat has such a significant edge on the fleet that they can tack early, so an early start usually means going pretty hard left up the beat, which is high risk.

It often pays to start earlier in light and shifty winds as the pathfinder typically has to sail through confused wind and water as some of the fleet inevitably end up high of the line in the shifty wind.

If you are going to start late, ensure that you very precisely watch the time passed after the start and give yourself at least 15 seconds of leeway on the gate closing time to avoid taking an unnecessary risk with the gate closing or a late starter pile up. However, if everyone avoids a late start there could be perfect clear wind and water by pushing the start a little later!

Where to Sit Pre-start

In the pre-start period sit just above the gate boat's layline. A typical routine will be to beat from the start buoy at the 5 minute gun and stop about halfway along the gate, e.g. 2 minutes for a 4 minute gate. Then sit just above the layline. This ensures that you won't get caught out late if the wind lifts on port. As the start gets nearer, you should track back to a few boat lengths below the expected layline but stay highly aware of any windshifts or changes in direction of the pathfinder, especially in an unstable breeze. If you are unsure whether you are high or low of the gate, sheet in upwind on starboard and look at the bow of the gate boat. If you are gaining land or horizon versus it, you are crossing ahead. If you are losing land / horizon versus it, keep sailing fast because you are late!! (This is also a useful trick upwind for knowing where you are versus the fleet or to decide if you are crossing someone.)

Continue to track the breeze. If you find yourself headed on starboard, you should consider moving up the line to take advantage of the gate boat lifting and subsequent lift back (assuming an oscillating breeze and not a persistent shift). And consider heading down the line and starting earlier if you find yourself lifted on starboard.

In patchy wind, starting in a lull is a nightmare as you will find the boats starting before you able to cross you and you will also potentially be rolled by the boats above you. In this breeze, it is key to try to start in pressure. This is not easy. Be prepared to move up or down the line to start in pressure and ensure that you have your head out of the boat in these conditions, looking at what pressure is coming down the race course.

Just as for a line start, you should be working a gap to leeward in the last minute before the start. As you approach the start try to slow up the boats to windward to increase your gap to leeward, while being mindful that no one ducks your stern and takes your leeward gap. You should aim to keep your windward boats overlapped to prevent that happening. You need to be careful how aggressively you pursue this as you can win the battle but not the war! You can do a great job of holding the pack up above you but if you cause a pile-up you will often become entangled yourself. You will be in the right but that won't help your start, and there is no redress for someone infringing you. The offending boat or boats may take turns but you've still got a lousy start!

Again, earning a reputation for being a tough starter at training events is a sound investment as people will seek to start nearer slower, easier boats which creates space for fast, aggressive starters.

The Start

If you have created space, approach the gate on a close reach. You should cross the stern of the gate boat closely (how much you push this depends on your attitude to risk in that race) and use heel and sail trim to luff to a close-hauled course as you round the gate. If you can, you should give an early squeeze to windward to create a gap to windward to open up early room to tack. Sometimes you can catch the stern wave of the gate boat to gain a kick to windward. It is usually the boats who are able to tack first and start working the shifts who are the leaders at the windward mark.

After the Start

There is a lot more leverage on a gate start than a line start. So, if you get a good start, it is important to consolidate early by tacking across the fleet on the first small shift if you are to the left of the pack, or driving low and fast if you are to the right of the pack, depending on your first beat strategy.

Remember, if there isn't room to tack you can still work your way across the fleet by moving into high mode.

Mental Approach at Championships

The preceding chapters provide a detailed approach to championship sailing. At the event itself it is good to keep things simple and be comfortable with following your instincts. Your instincts are formed from your past experiences so are often right, even if you're not sure why they are right at the time!

Everyone is different, so everyone's approach to their mental game should differ. There are no right or wrong answers on this. Once you have mastered the technical aspects of a sport, it is said that 90% of winning is from the shoulders up!

The more you put yourself in high pressure situations the easier they become, because you get to know yourself better and learn how to handle the pressure.

Enjoying the Big Day

The stakes typically rise during a championship series until you reach the climax on the last day of the regatta where the whole event, or your outcome objective, may be at stake. These days don't happen often in life and, if you are in this position, it is undoubtedly well deserved after probably several seasons of hard work. So enjoy the moment!

Handling Nerves

You should expect to have nerves on the last day! Welcome them because they are a sign that you care. Indeed, if you have no nerves, it is probably time to take up a new challenge or sport!! Those nerves are part of the buzz of competing in any sport. It is how you react to and manage nerves that matters, not trying to stop them altogether (as you won't achieve that – which may worry you more!).

Welcoming them is the first thing to do. Then distracting the nervous part of your brain with activity can work. There is a huge amount going on before and during a race, so there is plenty with which to distract the mind. For example, what is the wind doing? What is the tide doing? Does the rig look right? And so on. It can help to put your tiller behind your back (the 'frying pan' grip) to dampen your steering and ease your sheets a little if you are tense.

In the lead up to high pressure races it is useful to have a set of pre-start and boat handling routines, so if negative thoughts or nerves start to jangle, you can fall back on these well-rehearsed processes to quickly fill your head with positive sailing thoughts.

Psyching Up or Down

Depending on the boat, it can pay to vary your mood to the day's conditions. It can pay to be angry in windy weather in boats where physicality works, or be relaxed in light winds. It is worth having a set of thoughts in your mental locker that wind you up or down.

Replacing Negative Thoughts

We all have negative thoughts to some degree and seeking to block them will not work as you cannot stop your brain whirring altogether! Seek to replace a negative thought immediately with a positive one. Think of all the time you have put in, when you have been fast in these conditions, all the perfect windy gybes you've pulled off, and so forth.

BRINGING IT ALL TOGETHER

PART 5

10 Point Plan for Helming to Win

Here are 10 key pointers to enable you to helm to win:

 Sail with the **best crew** possible.

 Copy the **static settings** and **kit** of the top boats.

 Work through the **dynamic settings** to find the **key 1-3 levers**. Initially experiment with a big range of settings, then narrow that range with time.

 Explore **pinching** and **free upwind grooves** and **downwind angles**.

 Pressure test **boat handling**.

 Practise **slow speed boat handling**.

 Pressure test **starts at training events**.

 Practise **two-boat tuning at close quarters**, making life hard for yourself, to increase your ability to sail in **narrow lanes**.

 Once you have done all of this, go back to the **finer tuning** – static settings, the non-key dynamic levers, try new kit.

 Get very **fit**!

And finally, I wish you happy sailing, but please don't beat me!

Nick Craig

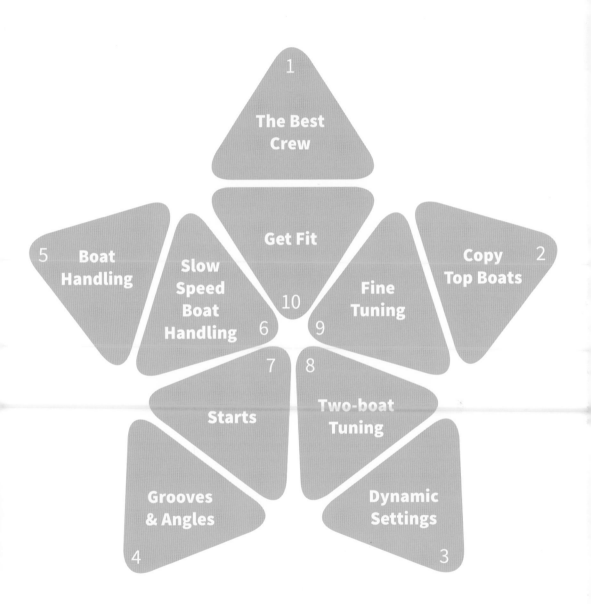